BOB WILLS
HUBBIN' IT

BY RUTH SHELDON

INTRODUCTION BY CHARLES R. TOWNSEND

Country Music Foundation Press
Nashville, Tennessee

Country Music Foundation Press
4 Music Square East
Nashville, Tennessee 37203

© 1995 by Country Music Foundation Press
All rights reserved.
Printed in the United States of America

Published privately in 1938 as *Hubbin' It: The Life of Bob Wills*
by Ruth Sheldon

Library of Congress Catalog Card Number: 95-068520

ISBN 0-915608-18-9

CONTENTS

INTRODUCTION

Iirst of all, I want to thank the Country Music Foundation for asking me to write a few pages that will introduce you to Ruth Sheldon's *Hubbin' It: The Life of Bob Wills* (as originally titled). I thank the Foundation, mainly, because this new edition affords me the opportunity to mention how Ms. Sheldon's book influenced my own life. The story is remarkable but a bit eerie. If there is such a thing as destiny, then I was destined to read her biography of Bob Wills. You might say the first book I ever read was Sheldon's life of Wills. By the age of eight I had read *Dick, Jane and Spot*, and I had given a cursory reading to Matthew, Mark, Luke, and John. I just did not like to read. In 1938, *Hubbin' It* was advertised on Wills's noon radio broadcasts over KVOO in Tulsa. Our entire family loved Bob Wills's music and would have loved to have seen the book, perhaps even own it. But the price for the book and a framable photo of Bob was $1.00. That was a day's work in 1938, and my father was out of work, dying of tuberculosis. My oldest sister had married a lawyer in Louisiana—and had money. She bought the book for my father, and he read it before he died, in the year of its publication, 1938. Other than the Bible and some *World Books*, Sheldon's was the only book in our home. Oh, I hated to read, but for Bob Wills I risked the pain. Happily, it was not painful at all. I loved it! Little did I know that thirty-nine years later, I would write the next biography of Wills, San *Antonio Rose: The Life and Music of Bob Wills* (Urbana: University of Illinois Press, 1976). Enough to make one believe there is destiny.

I still own that family treasure that I read at age eight while growing up on my granddad's ranch near Nocona, Texas. *Hubbin' It* has long been out of print, and we are all indebted to the Country Music Foundation for making it available once again. Ruth Sheldon was decades ahead of the times in writing this book. If she was not the first to write a biography of a popular musical figure, she was among the first. This is especially true for biographies in what was later called country and western music. That she could have anticipated Wills's star rising to the extent it did and that she judged the thirty-three-year-old

INTRODUCTION

bandleader worthy of a biography is phenomenal. Yet with the exception of the fans who purchased it in the late thirties and early forties, the book, which had been privately published in Tulsa, was almost forgotten until the revival of western swing music in the seventies. Interest in *Hubbin' It* since that time reflects a growing sophistication in both fans and scholars of American music.

It is not clear why Ruth Sheldon wrote the book. Her "Author's Note" says that she was a reporter for the *Tulsa Tribune* and had become interested in Wills when she wrote a feature article on him. Out of that initial article came the idea for *Hubbin' It*. Like many writers, she may have been looking for a subject for a book and had the intelligence and vision to see in Wills the ideal subject. When I was researching my biography of Wills in the early seventies, she told me that she and Wills had collaborated on the work as an image-builder to enhance Wills's career. It could be that fans, family, and friends suggested the need for a biography. From my own knowledge of Wills's mind, I think one thing is certain. The idea did not come from him. He was much too humble to have even thought of a biography of himself and most certainly would never have suggested it. Even in the early seventies after he had become an internationally known figure, at the time I was interviewing him for my biography, he never once indicated he was worthy of a biographical study. I have always believed the reason he allowed me to interview him on numerous occasions and write the book was that he wanted someone to talk with him about American music (he had suffered a stroke and was bedfast at the time).

Even a casual reading of *Hubbin' It* reveals Sheldon's intention to promote and further the career of Bob Wills. She did this in two ways. First, she employed an approach that had been successful in American literature in the nineteenth century. Furthermore, it was part of the American tradition and the American dream—that is, the rags-to-riches phenomenon in American history. The very name of the book connoted the hard economic struggle of Bob Wills and his family—and, for that matter, the difficulty of most Americans during the Great Depression.

INTRODUCTION

(The slang term "hubbin' it," which Wills used as a song title, originally described the difficulty of a wagon on a muddy road or in deep sand, bogged down to the hub or axle.) In a sense, Sheldon's book was good therapy for most Americans who read it at the time. Its message was clear: If a poor, uneducated boy such as Jim Rob Wills can be successful, so can countless others. Ruth Sheldon's thesis was to turn Bob Wills into the perfect example of a Horatio Alger story. Wills was an ideal candidate for such an approach.

Wills was also ideal for another theme in *Hubbin' It*, a theme that reflects a good deal of American thought in the thirties, and perhaps the thinking of Ms. Sheldon also. It was as if she applied the thesis of Matthew Josephson's *Robber Barons* (1934) to the life of Bob Wills. She did this very successfully by pitting W. Lee O'Daniel and the Burrus Mill & Elevator Company against Wills, who had worked for O'Daniel and the Mill in the Light Crust Doughboy band (1931–33). Thus, the lines were clearly drawn: rich, powerful, ruthless Burrus Mill and its president versus hard-working, struggling, powerless, poverty-stricken Bob Wills. For example, Sheldon wrote of Wills's struggle with O'Daniel and Burrus Mill when he left the company in 1933. She quoted Wills in an argument with O'Daniel over the inability of a band member to pay a grocery bill: "If some of the people wouldn't take all the big salaries and give us workin' people better wages, we wouldn't have to fight to pay our bills. We could live decent." Wills added: "I'm not going to bother you. You're a million dollar corporation. You don't have to make any explanations to a man who ain't got nothin'." After Wills left Burrus Mill, he advertised that he and other members of his Texas Playboys were "formerly the Light Crust Doughboys." O'Daniel and Burrus Mill sued Wills for $10,000 for using this advertisement. If they had won the suit, it would have ruined Wills. Of the trial, Sheldon wrote, "O'Daniel was present with a battery of lawyers from Fort Worth and Dallas." Wills could not afford experienced counsel and had to settle for two lawyers just out of Baylor University's School of Law. The account of the struggle between Wills and Burrus Mill continues

Introduction

through the end of *Hubbin' It*, and Wills's final victory (Tenth Court of Civil Appeals, 1935) offers a sort of climax in the biography. Without doubt, the drama of Wills's rags-to-riches story is heightened by its setting in the Great Depression and his battle with the Burrus Mill robber barons.

Sheldon told me that Wills's image, and not an objective account, was her principal concern. She emphasized only Wills's better qualities: his kindness to family, his generosity to anyone in need, his humility, his hard work, his common sense, his innate intelligence, his religious faith, and his forgiving spirit (even toward O'Daniel and Burrus Mill). She failed to discuss his drinking problem, which was the real reason O'Daniel fired him. Nothing was said of his miserable personal life that included several marriages and divorces. To paraphrase a popular song, she accentuated the positive and eliminated the negative. Though Wills did have all the admirable qualities she emphasized so very well, he had some less admirable traits as well.

This does not mean that *Hubbin' It* is not of value as a Wills biography. Even if she emphasized one side of Wills's life, her work remains useful. In my research, I found the facts, details, stories, and accounts of Wills's life, with few exceptions, correct and reliable. One reason for the book's factual accuracy is that Sheldon discussed many aspects of Wills's life with him shortly after the events occurred. In many instances, she was at a disadvantage because she had to rely only on what Wills told her. Nevertheless, when I researched many of the events and persons she had discussed, I found her work to be accurate. For the years she covered, from Wills's birth in 1905 to the book's closing in 1938, her biography is a very good primary source and an excellent outline of Wills's early life. Much of *Hubbin' It* has already withstood the tests of time and research, and will always be of value both to scholars and fans.

Hubbin' It has two other qualities that must not go unheralded. The book is very well written—free of the jargon, technical terms,

INTRODUCTION

and pseudo-sophistication that too often permeate today's literature. After nearly sixty years, the book is not dated. Above all, Sheldon's work has that certain something that her subject Bob Wills had in his music—call it enthusiasm. Enthusiasm is rare in our literature today. That is the reason, Charles A. Beard said, there is very little history written that is likely to live beyond its first birthday. Furthermore, as Samuel Eliot Morrison wrote, not much that is written in history today would lead one to die for one's country or live a better life in it. Neither Beard nor Morrison was talking about the kind of writing one finds in Sheldon's biography. In Wills she had a great subject, and she gave his life the enthusiastic treatment it deserved. Her writing, in short, was inspired.

Sheldon was so inspired by Wills's life that she wrote very little about his music. Maybe she saw something in Wills that few writers and fans have seen. It was the man that was really important, not just the music. It was the man that somehow came through in his music.

Ruth Sheldon was a pioneer, a pioneer in the sense that years before other journalists and historians she saw the importance of popular music in American history and culture. She mapped the trail that other generations of writers have followed. Like all pioneers, she took the wrong path here and there, and of course made mistakes. That is only natural and is one of the hazards of the trailblazer. Those who follow can profit from the missteps of those who forged ahead before. But moderns, regardless of their achievements, would do well to remember that those of us who follow are never quite as intrepid as the pioneer.

I think Ruth Sheldon's *Hubbin' It* inspired me back in 1938 growing up on that Texas ranch. I doubt if I would have written my own biography of Bob Wills had I not read her book in my early years. I owe Ruth Sheldon a debt I can never fully repay. I hope, if she read my book, that she saw her own influence and felt that I had at least partially repaid that debt.

—Charles R. Townsend

KVOO

PHILTOWER · TULSA

April 19, 1938

Mr. Bob Wills
Sains Academy
Tulsa, Oklahoma

Dear Bob:

Just a few words of good wishes on your proposed book
regarding your life, and experiences, which I understand is
to be entitled "Hubbin' It".

Well do I remember the day you walked into KVOO in February
1934 with an orchestra and a dollar and a half. We may have
needed the dollar and a half but we didn't need an orchestra.
Selling me on the idea that our public was interested in a
group of Texas kids with no particular claim to glory, was
not easy as you may remember. When I finally relented, due
entirely to your superlative ability to sell yourself, there
was considerable doubt in my mind.

Now, after four years of daily programs by Bob Wills and His
Texas Playboys, I am convinced that you knew exactly what you
were talking about when you said you'd prove a success.

I wish you and your book every possible success. When it
comes to "hubbin' it", Bob, I'll recommend you as the world's
champion. At this time I would like to be the one to make
a prophesy. If you sound as well in print as you do on the
air, your "hubbin' it" days are over.

Very truly yours,

W. B. Way
Vice Pres. & Gen. Mgr.
Radio Station KVOO.

WBW:g

The Most Powerful Station between St. Louis, Dallas and Denver
OWNED AND OPERATED BY SOUTHWESTERN SALES CORPORATION
EDWARD PETRY AND CO. INC. NATIONAL REPRESENTATIVES

AUTHOR'S NOTE

It is easy to know many people, but it is hard to know any one person. Usually when I have scratched below the pleasant, casual surface of an acquaintance I have been thoroughly disappointed, for I have had a number of nice, gullible illusions thrown right out the window. Contrary to the effect that sort of thing is supposed to have it has *not* made me cynical. It has just made me more eager to scratch a lot of surfaces in the hopes of finding some that will be more interesting and likeable the deeper I go.

It's like drilling oil wells . . . you make a lot of wildcat plays and get nothing but dry holes, but once in awhile you do hit a producer. Bob Wills is one of the best producers I have ever struck.

I first met Bob over a year ago when, as a reporter for the *Tulsa Tribune*, I interviewed him for a feature story. "There's a guy here that plays the fiddle and has a band that gets a thousand fan letters a week," my city editor commented in giving the assignment. "You'd better go over and see what he's got."

After talking to Bob for ten minutes I had an idea what it was he had. The longer I listened the surer I became. I couldn't describe it. Part of it was what made fellows like Lincoln and Will Rogers famous. Call it "the common touch" if you like. The term has stood enough abuse, but, at that, it is better than most to describe that special intangible quality. Besides that, there was something else. Maybe it was just that he was a real fellow.

Of course, I had thought before that people were first rate and then they would do something that would make them seem more like heels, but I was pretty convinced about Bob. I saw him frequently in the following months and watched him play for dances. I saw the expression people had on their faces when they looked at him or talked about him. He had already told me enough about his past for a newspaper story, but the more I talked to him, the more interested I became in the details of the things he had done and the way he felt about them. Also, the more convinced I was that he was a real fellow.

These things fascinated me and I suggested to Bob that they would be of just as much fascination to all the people that flocked to him wherever he went or wherever his music reached in the air. He said, yes, they were always asking questions about his life, but, of course, there wasn't enough time to answer.

1

HUBBIN' IT

So we began. Usually the toughest problem of a biographer is to get to know his subject, but mine was in getting my subject to stay put long enough to talk to him. He is always as busy as a rabbit with a coopful of carrots. However, when I could corner him, he would seem to slip into a trance and, forgetting that I was there, probe deep into everything that had happened to him and all that he thought. There was nothing that he withheld. I came to know him almost better than I know myself. The more I found out the more I admired him for what he is and what he has come through.

He has a remarkable memory. Not once have I had to manufacture a little detail here or one there to make a scene seem real. Bob supplied them all. When I commented on this faculty of his, he smiled and said, "Well, I didn't have no education. I had to use my mind somehow."

In discussing the book, Bob has often said that he hoped for one thing above all—that it will be a book which parents will want their children to read. The things that have happened to him could happen to many youngsters. He feels so strongly that it might have been easy enough for him to turn into an outlaw that he would like young boys to know why. It might lead them to be more careful and to think a little harder before they do something.

I've tried to tell faithfully what Bob has told me. I have learned a great deal from him and I hope that others may be able to learn it, too, in the following pages.

Bob says that he has never met a good friend or relative in his life that did not want him to come see them, always adding, "Be sure and bring your fiddle."

But it is not the fiddle—it is Bob!

—Ruth Sheldon

Tulsa, Oklahoma
April, 1938

PRELUDE

*The frightened mules bolted around the corner. The hub
of the wagon wheel struck a huge rock and the buckboard
careened madly back and forth. The frantic driver, slipping
precariously from side to side, jerked the lines and pleaded
and bellowed. . . . He and the wagon were "Hubbin' It."*

The life of Bob Wills has been like that . . . meeting adversity at every corner.

Always he has been forced to do things the hard way. He came from a way of life that was like quicksand, treacherously and unrelentingly trying to suck him down into its oblivion. His struggle for freedom has led him to do and be many things—a cotton picker, preacher, hobo, carpenter, roughneck, surveyor, shoe shiner, insurance man, car salesman, barber, medicine show entertainer.

As unthinkingly as a man carries his nose on his face, he carried his fiddle in his hand through all his trials, never dreaming that one day it would be the instrument by which he could fulfill himself.

Bob Wills is not a great man, but he has accomplished a great thing. In a world where too much acreage is ploughed by shells rather than mules; where empty bellies, twisted minds, oppressed souls, enslaved bodies make the nightmares of sleep indistinguishable from the nightmares of wakeful living; where all these things exist, happiness is as elusive as an echo. Those who can make others joyous and carefree for even a little while today are giving as great a service to mankind as the scientists of many professions who fight to rid the world of disease, ignorance, crazy economic structures, and war. Bob Wills brings gaiety and forgetfulness to thousands of men and women with his music. There are many entertainers who have accomplished this, but few of them have the strong bond between themselves and their public that Bob has with his. Bob is still the cotton picker from Texas whose grammar was learned in the fields, although he has become the greatest entertainer in the entire southwest. He plays for the great mass of farmers and hard laboring men and women from whose ranks he came. Because he is still one of them, he knows what they enjoy and how to give it to them. Because they know all this about him, he is greater to them than any entertainer in the world.

There is the bond of "hubbin' it" between them.

CHAPTER ONE

A FIDDLER IS BORN

The doctor shivered as a gust of cold March rain blew in his face. His heels pressed sharply into the wet sides of his tired horse struggling through the sucking mud of the east Texas road. "The baby would pick a night like this to come in," he grumbled, straining his eyes into the stormy blackness that blotted out the sand jacks and scrub oaks that grew thick by the road.

A flash of lightning momentarily lit up with blue-white fire the lonely, rolling landscape. The sight of a small house ahead danced in the doctor's blinded eyes as a blacker night followed the crash of thunder.

A tall young man with worried eyes threw open the door and helped the doctor strip off his sodden great coat. "Doc, Emma's pretty bad," he said in a choked voice. "I was scared you wouldn't get here in time."

The doctor gave him the impersonal, tired smile that had been used to comfort many another young father made desperate by the trial of his wife's first baby. He quickly joined the woman and two men grouped around a bed in the next room.

"Aren't you ashamed of yourself, Emma, waiting to have the baby until a night like this?" the doctor said to the eighteen-year-old girl whose tortured tossing had knotted her black hair around her pretty face, now drained of color. Her smile ended in a grimace of pain and the doctor quietly set to work.

At one minute before midnight, March 6, 1905, an indignant squall drowned out the sound of wind and rain in the room and was followed by a triumphant cry from the young father, "It's a boy! We'll call him James Robert Wills like we planned!"

Twenty-two year old John Wills stretched out his arms for his first son as soon as he had been wrapped in warm, clean blankets. "I'm goin' to walk the floor with this fiddler," he exclaimed. "I'll make a fiddler out of you, son." His face glowed as he held it close to the red, screwed-up features of the tiny baby.

HUBBIN' IT

Emma's brother experimentally uncurled a little clenched fist. "He'll make a better fiddler than you, Johnnie," he commented. "Look at them long fingers."

The next day Emma smiled indulgently at her husband, who filled the shabby, little house with the sweet, melodious scraping of his fiddle, blending it occasionally with a high, piercing cry of his own. Their son was hearing his first fiddle music.

Perhaps the day old baby confused the shrill notes of his father's entertainment with his own bawling protests at being forced to begin life, where life was already so profuse and so difficult. There was no silver spoon waiting to pop into his hungry mouth to silence his cries. Instead there was the prospect of the drudgery, the heartache, the physical and mental starvation of a tenant farmer's family. There was just enough rented land to wrangle a one-horse crop of cotton and corn from the grudging earth. That particular part of Limestone county, Texas was poor country. Its people were poor. His father and mother were young, inexperienced and easy going. They were to have nine more children in rapid succession to complicate their struggle to make a living. There was plenty of cause for this first infant to cry about being born.

Yet the happy, lilting tunes played for him his first day of living soared above the inauspicious environment. Although he could not understand their secret meaning, they forecast a different life for James Robert Wills. His father's boast that he was to be a fiddler was a prophecy based on inevitability. This boy baby was the result of the union of the two most famous fiddling families in Texas—the Willses and the Foleys. Both his grandfathers had won the hearts of every Texan who heard them, by their mastery of the bow. Nine uncles and four aunts came in for their share of acclamation. His young father was already beginning to claim the honors of being the best fiddler in Texas. Fiddle playing was in the blood that made his little face so red as he gasped for breath.

There were other things that made his inheritance rich. The harsh, unconquerable, pioneering spirit that had brought his ancestors to Texas and enabled them to fight man and nature to keep their foothold . . . the stern pride that held their backs stiff and their mouths closed tight no matter

6

what the difficulty . . . the warm, generous love of family to the exclusion of all else . . . these traits were his, too.

There were no warring instincts in his nature of two strange families suddenly merged, for the Willses and the Foleys had grown up together for two generations. His great-grandfather Wills had been just such a country doctor as the one who rode through the stormy March night to administer to him. Doctor Wills had a big cotton plantation overrun with negro slaves. The problem of keeping them well fed caused him to hire an adventuresome, young Texan by the name of Foley, whose job was to ride the hills and prairies with his gun in search of game. Tasty wild turkey, succulent deer, pheasants, quail, wild pigs and small game were to be had in profusion. It was pleasant, easy work to spend the days hunting. Doctor Wills' son, who was the same age as the young Foley, accompanied him on his trips. They became inseparable companions. They married at the same time. When one wife had a child, the other did, too, until the Wills children counted up to 12 and the Foley children to 13. The children never really knew which family they belonged to, for both households were a mixture. Foley children lived with the Wills family for months at a time and Wills children lived with the Foley family equally as long. Their economic status was on a level by this time, for Doctor Wills, an impractical business man, had dissipated most of his plantation and upon his death, his son dissipated the rest.

It was thus that Johnnie Wills and Emmaline Foley grew up together. As a rejected suitor for Emma's hand commented upon their marriage, "Well, she was brought up to love Johnnie and he to love her." Johnnie and Emma had a special feeling for each other from the time that as a sturdy lad of five he watched her crawl around under the elm trees. When Johnnie was ten nobody was in doubt as to the way Emma felt about him, for when his father gave him a whipping for refusing to bring in the wood, Emma yelled louder at each stroke of the switch than Johnnie did. When he learned to fiddle he played only for Emma. There were other aspiring fiddlers who tried to win her attention, for she was one of the prettiest girls in the countryside, but nobody could play her favorite tune, "Sugar In The Coffee," like Johnnie could. They couldn't have married anybody else but each other.

HUBBIN' IT

Johnnie's hopes of raising their first son to be a fiddler were subordinated to the worry of just raising him for the first two months. Young James Robert did not seem to want to live. He was weak and sick. Not a day passed but what Johnnie was on his horse riding for Emma's mother, feeling sorrowfully sure that this time the baby really was dying. But the stock he came from was tough and hardy. The spark of it kept him alive until finally he became a normal, healthy baby, eager to get about this business of living even though it was to be a hard one.

His name was elastic. James Robert became Jim to his father, Robby to his mother, Jim Rob to his later brothers, sisters and friends. At various periods of his life he was dubbed Sport, Jim, Hot Shot, Jack and finally Bob, by which everybody knows him today.

He was a solemn baby. As he lay on a blanket in the shade of a brier thicket, he watched his father and mother picking cotton with not much laughter in his great, black eyes. It was as if he were contemplating how long it would be before he was out in the field helping them. It was not to be long. When he was five there were two girl babies, Ruby and Eloise, lying on the blanket and he was nursemaid. He had a little sack, a miniature of the big ones that hung from the backs of Johnnie and Emma. His inexpert, little fingers tugged at the white, fluffy pods. It was slow business filling the little sack for he stayed near the babies and looked at them twice to every once that he directed his attention to the cotton plants. If either of the babies moved or cried, he raced back to them.

It was a lonely life for the youngster. Their small farm was too far away from Kosse, the nearest town, for him to experience the delights of games with other children. There were none his age on the adjoining farms. However, there were a number of negroes living nearby. One afternoon his mother found him on his knees rolling two small rocks on the ground, snapping his fingers and moaning. When she demanded an explanation he said, "I'm playing like the niggers do."

"Do you want to be a nigger?" Emma asked him, after telling him that he was doing a wicked thing.

"No," he said. Before she could speak again he asked, "Will God forgive me if I ask Him to?"

A Fiddler Is Born

When she assured him that He would, Bob kneeled again on the ground, this time with his hands clasped together. In a few minutes he rose and said consolingly to his mother, "It's all right now. God forgave me and I won't do it no more."

That was the beginning of a strong religious sense which not so many years later was to influence him to become a preacher.

Bob's only real playmate was a little burro which he adored. Whenever he was not helping with the chores he was astraddle its back galloping around the farm. This was an infrequent pleasure as there was much work to be done. They all worked in the fields. Before Emma's marriage, she had won the title of the champion girl cotton picker in the county. Now she had to pick even faster, for there were the children to be taken care of, the meals to be cooked, the house and vegetable garden to be tended. She had a passion for cleanliness. Unless the children and the house were as immaculately clean as strong soap and water could make them she could not sleep. It was not too much for her to work in the fields from sunrise until sunset and then scrub floors, wash clothes and iron until after midnight. Although their possessions were few, her pride insisted that whatever they had should be as clean and neat as possible. Johnnie's work was no less arduous.

Just as the greatest craftsman cannot make a gold watch out of scrap iron, so, no matter how hard they worked, Johnnie and Emma could not make a good living out of the exhausted, inhospitable soil which composed their farm. There were four children by now and a fifth was on its way. Like the pioneers from whom they were descended they decided to migrate in search of that will 'o the wisp—a better chance.

In 1913 a covered wagon piled high with all their possessions and drawn by their work horse and mule headed west carrying Johnnie and Emma and three babies towards hopeful uncertainty. Behind the wagon trailed eight-year-old Bob mounted happily on his little burro thinking it a great and wonderful adventure. He refused to ride in the wagon with his parents although the little burro was not a comfortable seat for the steady plodding of mile after mile. Emma and Johnnie were worried about his health if he

9

continued to make the journey so strenuous. They argued with him until he consented to let them sell the burro. The rest of the trip was a sad one for him. He grieved for his lost playmate as though it had been human.

The humble little group traveled almost five hundred weary miles before Johnnie decided that they would stop to make a home again. They were in Hall county, about a hundred miles from Amarillo. Johnnie rented a small corner of one of the big ranches and started anew the old struggle with cotton, corn and fate.

It was an even harder battle than before. For the first time, the children learned what it was to have no food in the house when their young stomachs were clamoring for nourishment. One day Bob took the smaller ones into the field with him to work. They had had no breakfast. A meagre supper the night before had left them hungrier than ever. Johnnie had hitched his ploughing team behind the wagon and driven off before sun-up. The children were frightened and the pangs inside them were almost more than they could bear. When some neighbors came by and talked to them they said nothing, although it would have been easy enough to get food by mentioning their situation. They feared what their father might do to them more than they wanted to ease their hunger. Although Johnnie had never whipped them for anything, he had instilled his strong pride in their childish minds. Suffering was better than humiliation. They knew that they must endure whatever happened without talking about it. In the afternoon, Bob managed to catch a sluggish rabbit and made a little fire over which to broil it. They ate the badly cooked, unseasoned meat as though it were a rare delicacy. Even today, twenty-four years later, the memory of that unfortunate rabbit lingers with Bob as the most marvelous meal he has ever made. Late that night Johnnie returned without his team. He was tired, with a worried look in his eyes, but he had $50 worth of groceries in the wagon. They feasted. Bob was only nine years old, but he knew more than ever now how serious life really was.

In spite of Johnnie's encouragement and his heritage, the youngster had shown no interest in playing the fiddle. He did not mind listening to music, but he was indifferent to picking up the fiddle himself. His disappointed father managed to teach him a few chords upon the guitar. When he was urged enough, he would consent to accompany Johnnie's fiddling.

One hot summer afternoon, the year after they had come to west Texas, Bob was lying listlessly in the shade beside the house, listening in a bored fashion to his thirty-five-year-old cousin, Olford Sanders, trying to play a tune on a fiddle. It was a simple, little tune, but Cousin Olford was having difficulty. He had great ambition to learn, but no talent. Haltingly, he screeched out the notes over and over again. The bow skidded in his sweaty hand. Bob winced at every discord.

"Cousin Olford, I ain't never played the fiddle, but I bet I could play that tune better than you can!"

"You keep still, Jim Rob! You cain't play it."

"Well, I've listened to you try to play it enough so's I know how it should be played. Let me have that fiddle an' I'll show you."

"All right, Jim Rob. But I'm tellin' you. If you play it better'n I can, I'll never touch no fiddle again as long as I live!"

The feel of the fiddle seemed natural to Bob. Something stirred in him. He softly drew the bow over the strings. Then easily, sweetly, he played the little tune. Cousin Olford's jaw dropped. Bob was playing as his father played, as his grandfathers had played—with the sure mastery of an old time fiddle player. Bob played the tune again and grinned at Cousin Olford.

Silently Cousin Olford took the fiddle and walked away. He muttered incredulously. Never again did he attempt to play the fiddle.

Bob's interest in the fiddle died away as casually as it had been aroused. Occasionally he experimented with it, but there were other things to be done. He was learning to read and write in an isolated little schoolhouse bearing the gentle name of Friendship. He was only to finish the seventh grade because that kind of teaching did not seem as important to him as the things he learned while driving the wagon during the harvest, roaming the canyons, increasing his skill as a cotton picker, and talking to the hard-living, kind-hearted ranch and farm people whose friendship he won so easily. His babyish solemnity had changed only to a quiet sense of self-possession which made the handsome little boy stand out from the other youngsters. Already his leadership and his ability to handle people was showing itself, not only among those his own age, but among the adults as well. When the transient cotton pickers came to work on the farm, they accepted orders from him as well as from his father, for Johnnie encouraged his first son to mature quickly.

It was not until Bob was eleven that he thought of the fiddle seriously. His father was asked to play at all the ranch dances and would usually take Bob with him to strum the guitar. One day Johnnie told him to meet him at a nearby ranch house where they were to play and instructed him to bring the guitar and the fiddle.

Bob arrived ahead of time and waited patiently for his father watching the people gather and responding politely to their conversation. When everyone had arrived, he looked nervously around. Surely his father was there. Johnnie was not to be found. The ranch owner looked annoyed.

"Poppa will be here any minute," Bob protested. A half hour passed. Still no Johnnie. The crowd was openly complaining. They had come to dance and have a good time. How were they going to do it without any music? Nobody else could play. A few of the men who had been drinking freely were surly. There was sure to be trouble.

Bob tugged at the angry ranch owner's sleeve. "I know a few tunes on the fiddle," he said. "Maybe they won't mind my playing until Poppa gets here." The ranch owner was dubious, but something had to be done. He brought a little box for Bob to pat his foot on and waited for him to begin. The crowd was amused as the youngster put his bow to the fiddle, but as the tune poured out their feet began to tap. Soon everyone was dancing. Bob only knew six tunes, so he played them over and over. It was an exhausted little boy who put down his fiddle at 2 o'clock in the morning, but his eyes were bright with pride. His father's forgetfulness had forced him to play for his first dance and he had been a success.

CHAPTER TWO

ESCAPE FROM COTTON

The soft, white balls on the cotton plants in the fall of 1919 looked like pearls to the cotton farmers, for that year a bale of cotton brought $200. Johnnie Wills had a hundred bales. There was enough money for the family "to kindle fires with in the morning."

There were months of high living with good food, trips to town, new clothes. Johnnie ended his life of a rent farmer by buying six hundred acres of a ranch by the Red River, not far away. He bought eighteen wild mules to Bob's delight. Bob and his friends spent glorious days roping the mules and riding them just for fun. It was exhilaratingly dangerous. It also unwittingly taught him a new wisdom. Later on, he was to find that a dance crowd is strangely like a bunch of wild mules and requires the same quick, thoughtful handling. There were new horses to ride madly over the hills in pursuit of coyotes. The day that Bob roped one filled him with triumph.

The money was soon gone, but there was the new farm and an even bigger cotton crop to be had for the next year. When the fields were like whipped cream spread over the chocolate earth, the tramp cotton pickers came and were turned away. There was bitterness and a sense of wrong in Bob's heart as he helped his father plough under sixty bales of the most beautiful cotton they had ever raised. The bottom had fallen out of the market. Cotton was so cheap that they could not sell it for as much as it would cost to pick it. Where the blame lay, he did not know. He felt the tragedy of destroying what was good and useful, because a capricious economic system had sold them out. They were poor again. Did part of the fault lie with his father? He could not help the price of cotton, but did Johnnie Wills ever provide for disaster? Had the years of struggle, the knowledge that a farmer can never be sure, had these taught him to be shrewd? Bob's young mind wrestled awkwardly with these questions. He could not find the answers. He knew that his father always took the easy way, preferring to let things drift. He was a hard worker on occasion, but he lived from day to day instead of building for a tomorrow. When he was without money, he knew that he would not really suffer, because he could always borrow. Even the most miserly man dug deep into his pockets under the influence of Johnnie Wills' genial, persuasive personality. It was easy enough to borrow more before the first loan was paid back.

These things gave Bob a vague feeling of dissatisfaction. He felt that he did not really like the sort of life his family lived. There was nothing really wrong with it. He knew no other kind of life. He did not even know what else he would prefer, what else he could do. But there was a nameless emotion that added yeast to the resentment brewing in his heart.

Old Man Bridges helped it along, too. The tough, simple old man worked for Johnnie asking nothing but his room and board and an occasional bit of spending money. Sometimes when he was ploughing fields with Bob, he would stop to rest and yell for Bob to come to him. Raising a huge, bare foot, calloused by years of contact with earth and stone, he would strike a match on its sole and light his pipe. Cocking his big, fine head meditatively he would look at Bob and say, "Jim Rob! Look at this old head—bald as a rat. Look at these feet—tough as whip leather from bumpin' clods all my life. Son, don't you stay here on the farm, or it'll happen to you. You go away. There ain't nuthin' to be got from a life like this. Yore young. Yore smart, Jim Rob. You go do sumpin else. Don't you tell yore pappy I'm tellin' you this. Don't you tell him, but you go way."

Bob was sixteen now. He felt that he was a man. Old Man Bridges' advice burned in his thoughts. He made his decision. Without a word to Johnnie and Emma, he slipped away one day to the railroad and hopped a freight train. It was going east and as it rattled along uneasiness overcame him. He had never been away from home before. He had no money in his pockets. He had no idea where he was going or what he would do.

Late that night he swung off the box car at the little town of Mexia in east Texas. His exhausted body was crying for food and sleep. He was too proud to ask for food or money. There was no use trying to find a job until morning, so he curled up on the grimy depot floor to sleep. There were tears in his eyes, for he was blue and discouraged. He was still a little boy at heart.

On the station platform a frantic woman and her husband paced up and down. The woman was screaming hysterically. Their son and two daughters had been killed at the railroad crossing a few miles out of town and they were waiting for the passenger train to bring them the broken bodies. A few sympathetic friends had gathered and were also moaning and crying. This wild, unrestrained grief pierced the heavy sleep which had claimed Bob. Instead of awakening him, it wove itself into his dreams. It seemed to him that his mother was crying for him to come to her and screaming that her heart was broken because he had run away. He turned and twisted on the hard floor in agony.

The horror of the night was not dissipated by the dawn, but he did not think of going home. He had set out to wander and wander he must, until the restlessness that filled him was appeased. However, most important of all at the moment was food. He washed hurriedly in the station and went out. At every store where he stopped there was no work to be had. The morning passed. He felt weak. A man mentioned that a farmer seven miles out of town needed someone to help him. The seven miles seemed like seventy as Bob walked unsteadily along. When he reached the farm, he was told curtly that they did not need anyone. It was late afternoon. He had had no food for two days, but he still could not lower his pride to ask for help. His mind was numb now. He could not think straight, but he remembered the railroad track he had passed. He managed to catch another freight train. Twenty miles further on, he abandoned it, for he was in Farrar, where he knew that he had relatives.

Food, a good bed, and the hospitality of the family restored his self-confidence. They arranged for him to borrow a fiddle and play for a dance in the little town depot. He made $5. With this independence safe in his pocket he set out again. It was June and good to be alive. Sitting on top of a box car with the wind cooling his body, he felt happy. It did not matter where the train was going. He caught this one and that one, swinging off near an occasional little town to buy hamburgers. The $5 was soon gone, but the wheat harvesting season was beginning and Bob was sure he could earn money in the fields.

Hubbin' It

He found himself in Knox county, not so far from home. There was a German colony north of Munday and their fields were lush with wheat. They were hiring many men. They thought Bob too slight to do a man's work as he weighed only ninety-six pounds, but as they were short of help they hired him to pitch wheat. They were not ready for the pitching the morning that Bob went to work, so he chopped cotton until noon. The women brought great hampers of rich, heavy food for the noon day dinner and Bob ate heartily. The day was oppressively hot and he wished that he had not eaten so much as he began to pitch the stacks of wheat up on the wagon. He worked vigorously, for he was determined to show the men that he could work as well as any of them. He wanted to keep the job during the season. The big, heavy-set German boys noticed how hard he was working. Grinning maliciously at each other, they began stacking up double loads for him to pitch. The wheat was thick and making forty-five bushels to the acre, so that the bundles were heavier than an ordinary man would attempt to lift. In his frenzy of work, Bob did not notice the uncouth joke they were playing on him. His body did, for suddenly, unable to stand the strain of the work, the enormous meal and the heat, he keeled over in a faint.

A splash of water in his face brought him to consciousness. He looked weakly at the boss man, who said angrily, "You're too small to work. You're fired. Now I gotta go get another man."

Bob followed him to his car and asked if he might ride with him to the main road. The man merely grunted and Bob got in. At the road, the man stopped, not offering to take him any further. As Bob turned away, the man said curtly, "Here, you was hired for $2 a day. So here's a dollar."

"No, sir. I don't think I should take it. I've caused you a lot of trouble to go get another hand."

The man stuck the dollar bill back into his pocket and without another word drove off. Bob clenched his fists in his empty pockets and walked down the dusty road, his head held stiff with pride. It was five miles before he came to a little country store. He asked the store keeper if he knew where work was to be had. He pointed to a woman in a buggy preparing to drive away. "I heard her say her husband was lookin' for someone to help him chop cotton," he said.

ESCAPE FROM COTTON

The woman cautiously told him that maybe her husband was looking for someone. If he liked, he could ride to the farm with her. Bob accepted gratefully. The five mile walk had drained his last energy reserve. When they reached the farm she told him her husband was ploughing in a field a mile from the house. Bob, still weak from his fainting spell, managed to drag over the distance.

"Well, I do need some help choppin' my cotton for a few days," the farmer said, looking him over. "But I couldn't pay no more than seventy-five cents a day."

Bob's eyes clouded angrily. That was just half the cheapest price paid for labor. "I was makin' $2 a day at my last job choppin' cotton and pitchin' wheat," he protested.

"I cain't pay no more. If you want to take it, all right. But if you don't, you'd better be headin' towards town. It's purt near sundown."

The possibility of more walking made Bob no longer care about money. At least, he would not have to work any more that day and could get a good supper and go to sleep. If he could only rest! "I'm worth more than that to anybody, but I'll take it," he said quickly.

The farmer handed him the lines saying, "Here, you take this mule and finish the ploughin' and then come in to supper."

The mule had never ploughed so fast in its stubborn life as it did under Bob's exasperated driving for the rest of the afternoon. When he stumbled wearily into the house, the farmer's wife asked him to draw some water. He figured that well must have been a thousand feet deep, for the bucket did not seem to get any nearer the top no matter how much he hauled.

A baby was crawling around the kitchen floor crying lustily. The farmer's wife picked her up and thrust her in Bob's arms. "You hush her while I finish fixin' supper," she said. As Bob rocked the squirming, squawling infant, he felt he could stand no more. He was so worn out when supper was served that he could scarcely force the food into his mouth. The pallet spread on the kitchen floor for him a little later seemed like a feather bed as he quickly lost consciousness.

The next morning was Thursday. Although he had been hired to chop cotton, the farmer was bent on having him do all the work, so Bob ploughed during the morning. There were fifteen acres of cotton to be chopped which would take an ordinary chopper more than four days to finish, averaging three and a half acres a day. The well, the poor food, bad pay, nursemaid duties, the lazy farmer, all melted into such a strong desire to leave as quickly as possible that it made Bob an extraordinary cotton chopper. He attacked the plants as if they were a vast nest of rattlesnakes threatening his life. The farmer watched him with amazement, as he flayed his way through acre after acre. "Boy, you'll kill yourself if you keep that up," he commented.

"Listen, mister, if I finish this by Saturday noon will you pay me off and take me into town?" Bob asked grimly.

"Well, yes, I would, but I ain't a-goin' to have to do it, for no human could finish in that time. And I ain't a-goin' to pay you if it's not chopped right neither."

"It'll be chopped by then and it'll be chopped right. You just follow along and see for yourself."

The farmer grudgingly admitted that the chopping was perfect. However, he protested that Bob could never keep it up. Bob said nothing. His speed and accuracy did not slacken.

As the sun climbed high Saturday, there was less than an acre to finish. "You go back to the house and have your dinner and wash up and be ready to take me to town," Bob yelled. "I'm goin' to have this finished." Finish it he did.

There was little conversation between the two as they drove into town. Bob's efforts had been as much of a strain on the farmer as they had on himself. Each was glad to be rid of the other.

As they joined a crowd of farmers exchanging the week's gossip in the depot, they heard a big, hearty man asking if anyone knew where a good hand could be found. Bob stepped forward boldly saying that he was a good hand.

The big man looked with amusement at Bob's slight frame drooping with weariness. "So you want a job, son. Now just what could you do?"

"Most anything," Bob said shortly.

"He's the workingest kid I ever seen," his ex-employer volunteered and told of Bob's accomplishments in the cotton field.

"You're hired," the big man said. "I'm Roscoe Potterage and I'll be in to get you Monday morning."

Bob was up before daylight Monday morning. He was so eager to start his new job that he didn't wait for Potterage to come for him. Instead, he walked the seven miles to the farm. Potterage was too busy to tell him what to do at the moment, so Bob asked Mrs. Potterage for a hoe so he could do some chopping for her in the garden.

"Well, if you want to work that badly I'll give it to you," she said, smiling kindly and approvingly.

Bob's working frenzy still possessed him when he joined Potterage in the harvest field. He pitched wheat with the same determination which had caused his fainting a few days before. Potterage watched him awhile and then called him aside.

"Listen, son, there ain't no point in workin' so hard. Now, take it easy. You'll get more work done in the long run. I ain't goin' to have you kill yourself workin' for me."

Bob gratefully slowed down. Potterage beamed encouragingly.

The Potterages had no children and as the harvest days wore on they began to lavish affection on Bob as though he were their son. They were religious folk and took him to church and revival meetings. Their kindly, simple talk about God and a man's duties to God and his brethren stirred deep in Bob. He thought of these things as he once had when he was a child. He regretted his boyish thoughtlessness and mournfully catalogued the things that he had done which he considered sinful. As his body grew strong and muscular with the steady work in the fields, his mind also grew strong with the conviction that he must be one of the chosen ones called to preach the gospel. He would dedicate his life to God. When he told the Potterages, they nodded approvingly, and listened proudly as he arose in the simple gatherings of the farm folk and preached to them.

Bob felt this "call" more strongly as the winter passed and spring turned into summer. The next fall when the cotton had been picked and there was little work to be done on the farm, Potterage had a serious talk with him. He and Mrs. Potterage wanted to send Bob to school and make it possible for him to graduate from a seminary so that he would be fully equipped to preach anywhere. Bob had left home to find a different sort of life. Here it was stretching out its hands to him. He could have a fine education. He could do a great work. There was everything to lose if he should refuse. He hesitated. That ancient pride, which had made him go hungry and had made him suffer, was persecuting him again. His craving for independence and his unwillingness to have anything done for him that he did not work for with his own hands, were fighting his desire to accept. These people had been kinder to him than any had ever been before. They loved him and were willing to work so that he might go ahead. But Bob could not let them. If he were to amount to anything it must be through his own efforts. He did not want to be obligated to anyone. The Potterages were sad when he told them that he thought it best to go away and find something else to do. They did not want to lose him, but because they loved him so much, they were able to understand, at least a little, why he felt he must go.

His heart was heavy as he went away, but his body moved with a curious sense of freedom. He was wandering again in search of that something to satisfy the disturbance in his soul.

He walked and caught rides into Wichita Falls where he had determined to catch a freight train back home. It had been a long time since he had seen his family. He was lonesome for their strong, easy love. Perhaps, too, things might be different. However, he was not expecting too much.

A tough, young man joined him just outside of town as he waited for the freight train to come out of the yards. They chatted casually and ran together to swing onto the cars. Bob, whose experience with freight jumping was not that of the young man's, did not catch a ladder that went to the top of a boxcar. The one he found himself clinging to, as the train gathered speed, had only a few bars. There was no possible way for him to get inside the car, which was closed, or on top of it. He could not jump from the train, for it was going so fast by this time that a tumble down the steep embankment might kill him. He was thoroughly frightened. His body hung dangerously close to the wheel. The motion and speed of the train made it hard to hold on, and his fingers were quickly growing numb with pain. The young man, who was safe on top of the next car, realized his new companion's predicament and lowered himself as near as possible to the swaying coupling between the two cars.

"Kid, you'll have to jump for the coupling," he yelled. "And I'll pull you up."

Bob's stomach contracted with sick terror as he thought of the action. He had to do something. He could hang on only a few more minutes before he would be forced to let go. Suddenly, he flung his body with as much force as he had left and landed sprawling on the coupling. For one horrible moment his head almost touched the road bed and the hot cinders flew in his face. Then he regained his balance and grasped the young man's hand.

In a few seconds he was safe on top of the car, shaking with the terror of what had happened.

"That was a close one, kid," the young man said weakly. "I sure thought you was a goner."

They crawled along the train until they came to a flat car which looked like a Fourth of July picnic grounds. There were sixty-four men and boys sprawled over its dirty bottom. They had scarcely joined this crowd when one of the brakemen came swinging along. "Which one of you bums was the one that made that jump on the coupling?" he yelled.

"That was my buddy here," the young man said calmly.

The brakeman stared at the youthful Bob and cursed. "You'd better keep away from freight trains, boy," he said. "It was a miracle you weren't killed."

He made no effort to throw the gathering of hoboes off the train. Their number was a little startling to even the toughest railroad man. As the train slowed down over sixty miles later for a hill outside Childress, which was not more than thirty miles from Bob's home, everyone jumped off the car. They had told Bob that they would circle around town to avoid the authorities and catch the train again as it left town. Although Bob was not as enthusiastic about freight trains as he had been before, he decided to go with them. It was the quickest way to get home.

The railroad police had anticipated the men's plan. When they reached the point where the train was puffing slowly along they found nine police waiting for them. Bob, who was trying to be particularly careful about what ladder he caught, was the only one of the group who did not manage to elude the police and get on the train. He started to run with all the officers and a bulldog after him. Such an imposing array gave him the ability to jump a fence as high as himself. The police soon gave up the chase as they evidently decided it was not worth trying to catch one man when sixty-three had already escaped them.

When Bob reached the highway, a man in a sputtering car gave him a ride. As they jerked slowly along, Bob decided that it was a good thing he had not caught the train. He resolved never to ride another freight train. He valued his life too much. He was convinced it was a good thing he had not caught it when a few miles down the road they saw the entire group of hoboes limping along. They were badly beaten and bruised. Their clothes were torn to shreds. The train crew had been changed at Childress and the new members were as hardboiled as Texas railroaders ever come. They had roughly thrown every one of the luckless wanderers of the rails off the train.

It was a bad time for Bob to go home. The money from Johnnie's cotton crop was exhausted. He was borrowing to live on until spring. There were six children by now and a seventh expected. After the first few days of joyous reunion, he was more dissatisfied than ever. The year with the Potterages, during which he had led such a quiet routine and had been as good as his call to preaching told him he should be, had affected him deeply. He was a little shy of the heedless existence led by the boys with whom he had roamed the canyons before he left. Their drinking, dancing, fighting and going out with girls was repugnant to him. He classified those activities as sinful.

One evening, some of the boys persuaded him to go along with them to a dance. He had no intention of mingling with the crowd. He only wanted to be an observer. As they approached the house where it was being held, the sound of a fiddle floated out to him. He stopped. He had forgotten about fiddle music and had not touched a fiddle for a year. It seemed to him that it was the most beautiful sound he had ever heard. Each note was as sweet as honeysuckle, as soft as a colt's nose. Like a child following a Pied Piper, he was drawn by the magic music into the house. He forgot that he was clad in dirty overalls whereas everyone else was slicked up for a good time. He forgot that this was "sinful." He could only think how wonderful it was to hear such music. One of the girls came up to him and asked him to dance. Still entranced, he moved out on the floor and in a few minutes was whirling around and around. He had always been a good dancer and the girls flocked around him. They made him dance until he was exhausted. When it was over, he came back to earth with a sick thud. The realization that he had danced and enjoyed himself fought with his year's belief that he should not do it. The battle left him disgusted with his "weakness," but another issue of his life had been decided. He would never be a preacher.

There was nothing for him to do at home, so he left in search of work. He roamed up and down the country, working where and when he could. Fall found him in Quitaque, not more than twenty miles from home, pulling bolls for fifty cents a day. He already knew some of the young people there and it was not long before he knew everyone. He was always popular and he enjoyed the simple partying that went on. He saved his money carefully so that by Christmas time he had $17. He was pleased with his thrift until he began receiving presents from all his new friends. His pride would not permit him to receive without giving. He could not bring himself to give cheaply either, so he spent his entire savings for gifts.

After Christmas he walked gloomily down the road leaving Quitaque. Here he was again without money and prospects. After three years of being on his own he was in no better condition than when he first left home. As a matter of fact, he felt that it was worse, for he had a feeling of failure.

He walked five miles to a farm where he thought he might be hired to pick bolls, but they did not need anyone. He walked on. Night came and still he walked. It was cold. He knew of no place to sleep. Then he came to a one-room, broken hut by the side of the road and found that a man and his little boy, with whom he had worked in the fields before Christmas, had appropriated it. They had no cordial greeting for him and merely grunted a sour assent when he asked if he, too, might sleep on the dirt floor for the night. The next morning they fixed a meager breakfast, but did not ask Bob to share it. His neck stiffened and he left quickly. He had not seen food since the morning before. Hungrily he kept on down the highway and managed to catch rides on trucks into Amarillo. A big city is worse than the country for a hungry man who is too proud to ask for handouts. City people are too afraid of being imposed upon to offer hospitality if they suspect someone needs it. Bob was not worried. His sister, Ruby, had married and settled there. He knew she could give him a bed and food until he could be independent again.

There was little work to be found. He finally put a bit on his pride and held it in painfully while he borrowed $8 from his brother-in-law and bought a shoe-shining equipment. A man in a barber shop had promised to pay him a small salary to shine shoes if he would furnish his own outfit. For two days Bob lowered his eyes bitterly over dirty boots. Then he asked the shop owner if he could have a little advance on his salary. The man cursed him. There was no bit that could curb his pride at that moment and Bob walked angrily out of the shop. He was so embarrassed that he never went back to get his equipment.

In the early mornings, he had haunted the zinc smelter asking the supervisors for a job. They merely laughed at his persistence. Refusals elsewhere had made him desperate. The day after his ignominious departure from the barber shop, he was walking the streets despairingly. He passed the post office and idly looked at the brilliantly colored sign informing every passerby that he should "Join The Navy!" Bob had seen the sign before, but today he stopped in front of it. He looked at the picture of the handsome battleship set so serenely on impossibly blue and calm water. Why shouldn't he join the navy? Then the government could look after him. He would have no more worries. All this struggle for existence and indecision of purpose would be ended. He walked into the recruiting office and applied. Fortunately, they needed another man to complete their quota. They liked Bob's appearance. He passed the oral and physical examination.

"Well, boy, you aren't going to have any trouble getting in the navy," the officer commented.

Bob's eyes were frightened. This was going too easily and too quickly. Things were out of his hands. He began to doubt whether he wanted to dedicate himself to such discipline and orderly routine for the rest of his life.

"Excuse me just a minute," he said. "I left a friend out on the corner and I'd like to go tell him what's keepin' me. I'll be back in a minute."

Escape From Cotton

He almost ran from the office. Once again in the street, he felt that he had escaped from something dreadful. Suddenly, it occurred to him that it might be possible for him to steal a job at the smelter since they would not give him one. He resolved to try a ruse. If it did not succeed then he truly would come back and turn himself over to the navy. He would surrender to the discouraging thought that he could make nothing of himself and would give the navy a chance to see what it could do.

He borrowed a worn apron, saw, pair of pliers, and a hammer from one of his sister's friends. The next morning he arrived at the smelter with the regular workmen and fell in line with them. A new timekeeper was on the job and as the men went by took their names. He accepted Bob's name unquestioningly. The men were building a foundation for some large smelter buildings. The company was paying them well—$4.50 a day and sometimes as much as $6 for over time. Bob worked hard and at the end of the week received his pay just as though he had been hired. He reported for work the next week and still no one had discovered that he had stolen the job.

He worked steadily for six months, making money and building up a contentment with life. He paid back all his debts and was able to buy some new clothes. With this new prosperity was born a desire to fiddle again. He bought a fiddle for a few dollars in a pawnshop and played Saturday nights for small gatherings. He was happier than he had been since he left the Potterages.

A cousin came to Amarillo and, not liking city life, talked to Bob about the delights of being in the country. He told him how foolish it was to work so hard and be submerged with thousands of other people. Bob listened to him seriously. Secretly, he did long for the independence and individuality that the fields gave a man. It was fall. The weather was cool and he thought of the freshness of billowing fields of cotton, the absence of harsh noises. When his cousin proposed that they go to Knox county and pick cotton, he agreed to go. He realized that he was leaving a $4.50 a day job to work much harder for $1.50, but somehow he did not care.

Three days of cotton picking cured him. He was lonely and had lost the taste for it. Without explanations he left his cousin and went back to Amarillo. He discovered that thirty-six men had been laid off at the smelter.

Hubbin' It

Everyone told him what a fool he had been to leave and that now he would have no chance of getting his job back. Bob disregarded these commiserations and went to Lawrence Hedrick, the gang pusher, who had shown a liking for him. He told him he wanted to come back to work. Hedrick took him to Haines, the chief boss.

"What are you doing back here?" Haines inquired coldly.

"I want you to give me a job like a man for the first time," Bob explained.

"What do you mean for the first time? You worked here for six months and then quit of your own accord."

"I know, but I stole that job. Nobody hired me. I just took it and they hired me. But I want to be hired right and given back my same old job and my same old work number."

Haines' amazement slowly turned to amusement. "Well, what do you think, Hedrick?" he questioned the gang pusher under whom Bob would work.

"I think you should give it to him," Hedrick said.

"All right, Jim Rob. I'll give it back to you. You can have your job like a man now."

Chapter Three

Kicking The Traces

The years from 1921 to 1924 were particularly disastrous for the farmers. Many of them were reduced to living on bread and water and working their horses on grass. They would graze them half a day and work them half a day. But in 1925 there was a fairly good crop. Bob was weary of working in the smelter. He was twenty years old and in spite of all his experience was still pursued by the feeling that he had not yet found his niche in life. He decided to go back to the farm. Maybe that was where he belonged after all. Now that things were better he might have a chance to help his father work out a more secure existence.

All the extra money he had made had been sent to his family, so he returned as he had done before—without funds. His father was grateful that he had come back and gladly turned the management of the hands and the crops over to him. There was plenty of work to be done on the farm, but there was also time to play.

Bob had been away from home so long that the young men and girls in Lakeview, the town nearest their farm, did not accept him upon his return. They regarded him as a stranger and took the attitude that he would have to prove himself. This was a challenge which Bob wanted to take. He arranged with an old friend to give a dance and invite the local crowd. Then he went to Quitaque to round up his friends there. He arrived at the dance with eight carloads to find that the Lakeview crowd had brought their own fiddlers and were already dancing. However, Bob had brought Check Stocklet and his brother, whose reputations as players were at the head of the list in that part of the country. Bob played with them and they soon had the attention and admiration of the whole crowd. The Quitaque bunch followed Bob's instructions and ignored the others which annoyed many a Lakeview boy who wished he could meet a Quitaque girl and many a Lakeview girl who wished she could meet a Quitaque boy. After the dance, Bob's eight carloads had a breakfast and party all day Sunday, from which the Lakeviewers were excluded. This little proof of Bob's popularity elsewhere established him as the leader of the Lakeview boys, who sought his company after the episode.

Bob had accomplished what he wanted, but the incident had a much more important result. The crowd had enjoyed his fiddling so much that they demanded he play for them wherever he went. His reputation spread around the countryside and soon he was being asked to play at ranchhouses everywhere within a sixty mile radius of his farm. Bob still did not take his ability seriously, but he was being forced to play and to develop his talent.

It was not until he had attended a number of fiddling contests and won the majority of them that it occurred to him that someday he might organize a band. Even then, it was only a vague idea, for he thought that he would have to go to school and learn to be a director. He figured that chance would come in the far distant future, if ever. He was content, now, to have a good time with it. That he automatically was the leader of the players, no matter how many old fiddlers were at an entertainment, made no impression on him. He attributed it just to the fact that he was young and therefore could entertain the crowd better. He did not know that keeping the spirit of a party going is a gift which no school can supply.

During this summer he made a visit to his relatives in east Texas. The reputation of his grandfather and father, as fiddlers, had never been beaten in that part of the country. They had never heard Bob play, but when he did they went wild over him. Although Bob's technique and talent were no greater than his father and grandfather possessed, he had more showmanship. Bob never played sitting down, because he could not get the feel of the music if he did. He had to stand and sway his body with the rhythm of the melody. That was an innovation which they liked. They kept him playing all day and all night. They took him to their friends in all the surrounding towns. He played so hard and so much that his neck became bruised from holding the fiddle under his chin. The bruise became swollen and very painful, but Bob continued to play until a high fever stopped him. A doctor lanced the swelling and had to scrape his neck to the bone, for constant bruising and a bad case of varnish poisoning had developed into a severe case of infection. Before the wound was healed, Bob was playing again. He could scarcely keep on his feet because of the misery he underwent, but people were so eager to hear him play that he could not refuse. He held the fiddle tight under his chin, as he wanted to play for them as they expected him to play. He would not give them half measure by holding the fiddle in an easier position to the detriment of the music. He still bears the long, deep, white scars of this determination to plough over a difficulty.

More often than not, entertainments in Texas had the flavor of wild west days. A typical party of the period and the country happened during this visit. Bob persuaded two of his cousins to go with him to play for a dance in a nearby town. His uncle offered them $25 not to play. "Jim Rob, that's a tough town," he explained. "You'll get into trouble."

To a lad of Bob's headstrongness, that was the best reason why he should play for the dance. The cashier of the little town's bank appointed himself as Bob's host. Nothing was too good for Bob. The more the cashier drank, the more affable he became. The dance was being held in an abandoned frame church on the outskirts of the town. There was a large crowd and Bob was pleased to note the number of nice looking women present. He figured he would make a good sum from the dance.

The evening had only half progressed when suddenly the lights went out and there was a great deal of shooting. This did not upset Bob, for such a demonstration of high spirits was not unusual. When the lights came on there were no women to be seen. Bob went to the man at the door and asked how much money had been received. "Not any yet," the man replied. "They wouldn't pay."

Bob stalked back to the musicians' platform and told his cousins to put up their instruments. He was placing his own fiddle in its case when the affable cashier asked what was the matter.

"We ain't playin' no more," replied Bob firmly. "Nobody has paid and the evening's half over with. Besides, we don't play for no stag dances."

HUBBIN' IT

"This is one stag dance you'll play for," the cashier roared and ran to the door, pulling a long knife from his belt. "Anybody who tries to get out of here is going to get his!" He glared at Bob.

The lights went out again and a dozen fights started up around the room. Bob, still clutching his fiddle, made for the door. A big man in back of him said quietly, "Here, let me hold your fiddle while you sock that guy. He's asking for it."

Bob handed the fiddle to his ally and lunged for the cashier. The knife glittered and slashed from wrist to elbow the arm which Bob raised protectingly. Bob's other arm was not idle. He knocked the cashier backward down the three or four steps to the ground and plunged after him. He pounded the inert form upon which he landed until a weak voice came from it, "You're hittin' the wrong fellow! I ain't got nothin' to do with this!" It was a drunk who had passed out until Bob's blows brought him to.

The cashier was back in the doorway yelling for more trouble and looking for Bob. Bob's two cousins were lingering uncertainly on the fringe of the eagerly watching crowd in the room. They did not think it wise to brave the cashier's knife.

"Come on out of there, boys, and get in the car," Bob yelled as he grabbed the cashier and did a thorough job of taking all the danger out of him.

It was a subdued trio of cousins who returned penniless to face the uncle's "I told you so." Bob's ugly wound made fiddle playing out of the question for awhile. The town newspaper came out with a lurid story saying that Jim Rob Wills had nearly beaten nine men to death in the worst ruckus that ever happened in town history. Sometime later, Bob received a lengthy and abject apology from the cashier saying that it was the first time he had ever really been drunk and that he never intended to drink again.

Bob returned to the farm with plenty of scars to remind him of the country in which he was born, but he was due for another scar—one on his heart.

Before Bob had left home, one of the companions with whom he played in the canyons was a young girl. She was a quiet, little thing his own age. They had been sweethearts in a childish way. She rode horseback with Bob and liked the things he did. They often talked of what life would be like when they were grown and were confident that whatever it was, they would share it together. All the time that Bob was gone he thought of her. He built around her the rich, glowing idealism that is the stuff of storybook love. That he did not see her did not matter. She was one of his goals. Someday he would get straightened around and they could be married. She was the subject of many a beautiful dream.

Her family background was like his and, in her way, she felt the same dissatisfaction that he did. She dreamed of a life of security as every woman does, but her need for it was even greater, for she had never experienced it.

Her father took his family to Amarillo not long after Bob had been working there. He saw her a few times, but her family objected to him. They told her that he was not dependable and that she could make a much better marriage. Bob was not upset by this opposition. He was confident that her love for him was as strong as his. She would wait.

After his return from his east Texas visit he felt a great need to see her. He must talk to her, see how she was and reassure himself that all was well. When his father gave him $25 to buy a new suit, he decided to use the money to go to Amarillo.

The nearer he came to his sweetheart, the happier he was. Not far from her house he encountered her father. His greeting was so cordial that Bob was suspicious. The man had never concealed his dislike for him before.

"Well, Jim Rob, I spose you come to congratulate my daughter, didn't you?" he said maliciously.

"Congratulate her for what?"

"Ain't you heard? She's goin' to be married Sunday."

Bob walked a long time before he could bring himself to go to the house. He could not believe what he had heard. Surely she would not let him down like this.

She paled when she saw him. "Jim Rob, don't think badly of me," she said. "I can't help it. You don't ever seem to get settled down and make any money. I can't wait forever. I've got to think of the future. I ain't goin' to be like my family. I'm goin' to have things. I'm goin' to have a home of my own. A girl has to think about such things."

"What's the fellow like you aim to marry?"

"He's a good man, Jim Rob. He's a fellow here in Amarillo. He's got a job as a salesman and he makes good money. He'll take care of me. He loves me."

"But you don't love him!"

She was silent. Bob's eyes burned as he continued, "You love me and you always will love me, just like I'll always love you. Someday you'll find out you made a mistake. You can't treat real love like this. It don't pay. I can't say nothin' to you now, because I can't marry you like this fellow can. But you'll find out!"

Before she could answer, the voice of the young salesman was heard outside.

"Jim Rob, please go out the back way," she pleaded. "I don't want no scene."

"I'm goin' to wait right here. I want to see this fellow what's taken you away from me."

Nervously she introduced the two. The young man had heard of Bob and told him so, saying he was glad to have a chance to meet him.

"I'm glad to see you," Bob replied. "You know what kind of a girl you're marryin', don't you? She's the finest girl in the whole world. I know it because I love her and I've loved her ever since we were kids. They don't come no better. If you don't take care of her, well, I'll take care of you! I wish you both a lot of happiness."

The young man smiled seriously and held out his hand. "Thank you," he said. "I know that. You don't have to worry."

Bob said good-bye abruptly and left. Her father stopped him outside. "Jim Rob, I got to praise you," he said. "I didn't know you had it in you to be such a man."

Bob's manliness weakened under the pain he felt in his heart. The tears rolled down his face unrestrained as he walked away, headed back to the farm. He cried for the death of an ideal. He cried because he thought life had been unfair. He cried because he was hurt and felt sorry for himself.

By the time he reached the farm he had changed. He decided that since he had lost the one thing in life he really wanted, nothing else mattered. He knew that he could never love again as completely as he had this girl who was lost to him. His disappointment had released a wild thing within him.

Kicking The Traces

Although he could not forget, he was determined to live so fast and so hard that it would not hurt as much.

He began a period of his life that almost ruined him. It was easy enough to find tough companions to share the hardening of his emotions. Texas was full of them. They were fighting, drinking, unscrupulous fellows who loved trouble because of the synthetic superiority it gave them. They welcomed another recruit to their disorderly ranks and soon Bob was their leader. He proved he could out-fight, out-drink, out-trouble the most disreputable of them.

He forgot about the farm. He refused to think of his family. What was the use? What did he want security for now?

The Borger oil field was opening at that time and he decided that he could cash in on the boom, too—not by working in the oil fields, but by working the oil field workers and hangers on with his fiddle. A boom town pays high for entertainment and, besides, it would probably offer more of the excitement which he craved.

Toby and Roland, two of his gang, were ready to leave with him immediately. The trio started out late one afternoon in Toby's old car with only a few dollars apiece in their pockets.

"Now, boys, we're goin' to a tough country, so we've got to be tough, too," Bob cautioned them, feeling full of bravado.

About fifty miles from home they decided the time had come to put that advice into practice, for one of the tires blew out and the car limped on a rim into the little town of Goodnight. For the first time in his life Bob decided to steal. In their elated mood, the boys felt that there was no point in spending any of the small hoard of money on as expensive a thing as a tire.

A group of cars parked around a church looked like good pickings, so when Bob located a car like their own, he had the other two drop him by it. A street light directly over the car and the town telephone operator looking out of his office window a few yards away did not stop Bob. He calmly took the tools from under the seat of the strange car and jacked it up.

Toby and Roland had a little scheme of their own. They drove into a filling station down the street with the intention of giving a bogus check in exchange for a tire. The filling station attendant, who, unknown to the boys,

33

was the town law, figured something was wrong and made a point of opening the hood to copy the car's serial number.

This frightened Toby, who said, "All right, if that's the way you feel about takin' my check, I'll drive over to my uncle's and get the cash."

"That would be easier on both of us, son," the filling station attendant approved. "Where does your uncle live?"

"Oh, he lives on the right of the road a few miles between here and Claude," Toby lied. "I'll go see him."

As Toby pulled out of the station, Bob, busy taking the tire off the car, noticed the telegraph operator look at him intently and suddenly plug in the switchboard. This frightened him and he dropped the tools.

The filling station man and another fellow had climbed into a car by this time and were coming down the road after Toby and Roland.

"Jump on, Jim Rob," Toby yelled, but Bob made him come to a stop.

"What's the matter?" Bob asked, once inside.

Toby explained the situation as he drove out of town toward Claude as quickly as the old car would go on its one rim. "They're following us," he pointed out.

"Well, we ain't done nothin'," said Bob calmly.

They had not driven far when the car in back of them speeded ahead and stopped. The two men emerged with guns in their hands and stood in the center of the road.

"I'm going to drive right through them," Toby said desperately.

"No, you're not!" Bob shouted. "You want to get us killed? Besides, we can't out-drive them on a rim."

They stopped and the boys waited nervously while the men came to the car.

"Well, I thought you said you was goin' to your uncle's house," the law said, standing on Bob's side of the car and looking across at Toby.

"Sure, we are," Toby stammered. "He lives on down the road a piece."

"You've just passed the only house on the right side of the road between here and Claude," said the law grimly. "I guess you thought you could pull something in Goodnight, but we don't go for no rough stuff. And this fellow here was stealin' a tire off a car by the church. Well, it looks like I've caught myself a bunch of thieves."

KICKING THE TRACES

Bob suddenly threw his door open and leaped to the road facing the law and his gun with eyes blazing. "There ain't nobody, law or no law, that's goin' to call me a thief! I'm Jim Rob Wills from Lakeview and I never stole nothin' in my life. I sure didn't tonight!"

The law lowered his gun. "Why, Jim Rob," he said in a friendly voice. "I know you. Don't you remember me? You played here for Old Man Goodnight's birthday dance and every drink you had I give to you."

Slowly Bob recalled the occasion of a few months before.

"Listen, Jim Rob," the law said. "You boys was fixin' to get yourselves into a lot of trouble. Now, you go on, but you be careful and don't you try to do nothin' like this anyplace else."

A little later, as the trio drove down the road, Toby moaned, "Of all the luck! I never seen a fellow like you, Jim Rob. Why, do you know it was a thousand to one that law might've killed you when you threw that door open and jumped out. And him knowin' you! Of all the luck!"

But Bob was silent. The incident made him reflect. He had started to steal and his fiddle got him out of it. It was luck, yes, but luck does not follow a man's footsteps on every by-path. Bob thought a lot about that incident and never again in his life has he been on the verge of stealing. That night made him a little disgusted with the pig trough in which he was wallowing.

The rest of the trip to the Borger fields was a sorry tale. Two dollars in Amarillo purchased a tire that would do, but the entry into Pampa, the center of the boom, was as lacking in triumph as the entire stay. During Bob's thirteen days there he only had his shoes off twice—beds were that difficult to obtain. The dream of making easy money playing the fiddle exploded and one by one the boys went back to Lakeview. Naturally, Bob was the last to give up. Two weeks from his cocksure departure he was back on the farm.

Although he refused to think of it, the chances of his turning into a real bad man were ominously great. As yet, he had committed no crime, but the gang fights and trouble-making were laying a foundation for it. He had never known a genuine childhood. A good education and wholesome play had been subordinated by the necessity to work and shoulder responsibility when he was too young. He had received more hard knocks than the average youngster. Now he was determined to prove his toughness. Clyde Barrow, Pretty Boy Floyd and other wretched criminals had the same sort of background. The fellows he now called his friends were destined to clash seriously with the law. Two of them would be sentenced to life in the penitentiary. One of them was to be shot through the stomach by the police. Another was to serve a term in the penitentiary and be shot several times after his release. Bob was headed for the same thing.

His mother cried over him and prayed that he would change. His father argued with him. Bob would not listen. He did not care. He had established himself as the leader of these hoodlums and he intended to live down to the dishonor. Strangely enough, he was still received by the respectable people of the community. He was handsome and likeable. He could easily change to suit the people he was with at the moment. They knew what he did when he left, but they could not bring themselves to disapprove of him to the extent of refusing to have anything to do with him. Many a man and woman sorrowed over him as his family did and attempted to reason with him. He was a pet black sheep.

One of the more ruffianly of his comrades had a fight one day because someone made a disparaging remark about Bob. He lost an ear in the scuffle, a proof of his devotion to his leader. A few weeks later he walked up to Bob and pulled his cap down over his eyes. "I like you, Jim Rob," he said drunkenly. "I think you are as true as steel, but sometimes I think you are crooked." Suddenly, realizing what he had done, he apologized. Bob's face was white with suppressed anger as he snapped, "All right. Remember, though, I'm as tough as you and don't you try to pull nothin' on me, or I might act quick!"

It was not much of an incident, but a distaste for his companions was created in Bob and set him thinking.

Something else happened that impressed him. Jimmy was a tall, handsome, stalwart fellow. He was as quick to hit as any of the gang and as unruly. A carnival came to town and Jimmy's eye was caught by one of the girls. She was a flashy, peroxide blonde, but with a genuine prettiness about her. Jimmy, who was used to country girls, had never seen anything like her and she, who was used to the cheap riff raff of her profession, had never seen as fresh a complexion or as frank a manner as this country boy had. Jimmy made love to her and she returned it. They flaunted their relationship openly to the disapproval of the small town.

One afternoon, while Jimmy was waiting for her in front of the hotel he had a fight with a transient cotton picker. Bob and the other boys were an interested audience. The cotton picker, in a desperate attempt to get the better of Jimmy, bit his lower lip with such strength that it was torn completely off and hung from the side of his face by a slender thread of flesh. Realizing the enormity of his offense, the cotton picker crawled quickly away and disappeared. Jimmy stood up dazed, not realizing what had happened. The carnival girl stepped out and seeing the blood streaming down his mutilated face gave a piercing scream that could not have been more heart-rending than if she had practiced it all her life to deliver in one great moment. She was dressed in a white fur coat and hat and, to Bob, looked like a distressed angel as she held out her arms for Jimmy. He buried his face in her shoulder and his blood stained the white fur brilliant red while she sobbed over him.

The nearest hospital was thirty miles away. It was freezing weather. They put Jimmy in a car and the girl did not loosen her grip. She kept his face pressed to her as they sped over the road. The warmth of her body prevented the blood congealing and the doctors were able to sew his lip back in place so that in later life only a thin, white scar on his chin marked the accident.

That was the end of Jimmy's wild life. The carnival girl did not leave his side. Her devotion to him killed the gossiping of the townspeople who realized that she must truly love him. Jimmy and the girl were married and settled on a farm. Today they are staid, respectable folk who come to town only once a week and whose quiet life never gives a hint of their past.

These things disturbed Bob. Although he still considered that there was nothing in life worth bothering about, yet, perhaps the way he was living *was* wrong. He wanted to avoid an issue with himself, so without thinking it out, he abruptly deserted the gang and went into seclusion on the farm. For a few months he worked harder than he had ever worked before, helping his father with the crop. He refused to see anyone. He was silent with the family. He would not shave and grew such a beard that when he did go into town no one recognized him. He went to the barber shop and even the barber did not know him until he had shaved part of the beard.

In spite of this treatment his mind was still torn up. Out of sheer meanness he traded two of his father's good milk cows for a race horse that a passing Mexican offered him. Johnnie was furious and demanded that Bob get the cows back. "Them cows is mortgaged!" Johnnie exploded. Bob refused to get the cows and vented his restlessness on the horse. He ran him so much that he was soon convinced the horse really could race. He entered him in the county fairs and by betting on him ended in losing the horse, saddle and all the money he had.

The lack of money made him turn to his fiddle again. With a young fellow who played guitar, he stood on the sidewalk in Lakeview one Saturday morning and played. A crowd gathered, for no matter what they might think of Bob, they could not resist his fiddle. When he finished he passed his hat and collected $16 in coins. The pair rode to Lodge, nearby, and repeated their performance receiving about $8 more. They next drove to Turkey where they did good business getting $20 for their efforts. At Quitaque they only drew $7. So they hurried back to Lakeview and played a dance. At the end of a weary day they had about $30 apiece.

By this time Bob had sobered a little. He began to think again of his condition and the status of his family. After careful figuring of all the debts his father had accrued, the possibilities of crop returns, and what living expenses would be, he discovered that it would be ten years before they could pay their friendly creditors. He knew that bad crops and poor management would increase the debts even if they tried assiduously to pay off everybody. It was humiliating to him to associate with the nicer young people of the countryside knowing that his father owed each of their fathers from $5 to $5,000.

He was further humiliated one Saturday afternoon when he drove into Memphis with a group of young people. A horse race had been scheduled there between a local stallion and that of a traveling horse owner. The business men of the town had made up a large pool of money and it was a gala occasion.

KICKING THE TRACES

When Bob and his crowd arrived everyone was perturbed. The local horse had bucked off those who attempted to ride him and the race could not begin. Bob watched the men's distracted efforts casually, but suddenly he became intent. The horse looked familiar. He joined the crowd around it and scrutinized it carefully. When he saw that one of its ears was oddly scarred he was convinced. He had raised the horse himself and broken it. Many were the afternoons the two of them had galloped madly over the countryside. Then, during one of Johnnie's frequent hard-up spells, the horse had been sold.

"I'll ride that horse for you all," Bob volunteered. "I can handle him."

The men looked at him and laughed, but seeing that he was serious and determined to ride the horse, they drew him aside. "Are you drunk, Jim Rob?" they asked. "That's a bad horse. Ain't nobody been able to ride him, but he's a fast horse. We've got a lot of money bet on him and we ain't aimin' to have no fool lose it for us."

Bob persuaded them that he was neither drunk nor a fool, but he did not mention that he had raised the horse. He had as much difficulty in mounting as the others had encountered. In the struggle his trousers were ripped down one side. He managed to keep his seat and in a few minutes the horse responded to the long-forgotten voice and control.

Bob did a beautiful piece of riding and won the race. After the glory had subsided, he was painfully aware of the disreputable condition of his trousers. He had no money to buy another pair and the party his friends had planned was just beginning. His companions suggested he charge another pair at the general store so they could continue their fun. Bob was silent. He knew that his father owed a large bill at the store and the owner, although he had won money on Bob's riding in the race, would not give him any more credit. The girl whom he was escorting sensed the situation and drew Bob aside. She pressed a five dollar bill in his hand and told him to say nothing, but to buy the trousers. He argued with her, but she insisted. He bought the trousers. The shame of accepting money from a girl haunted him.

The temptation to return to a devil-may-care life was strong, although he realized that fundamentally it did not appeal to him. This time he faced the problem rather than attempting to run away from it. He decided that the fault must be within himself. Was he lacking in character? In the ability to change his life? No. He could do it. It would be hard. There were many difficulties to whip. Perhaps what he needed was a good wife to help steady him. Having the direct responsibility of another person would curb his instinct to shift with the wind in search of a better landing place. Yes, a fine country girl was the answer. He did not need to look for one. Already he had been paying respectful court to one whom he admired. The times that he had spent with her he had not been the Jim Rob Wills who could lick any so-and-so who cocked an eye at him. He had been the Jim Rob Wills that the Potterages knew—the Jim Rob Wills that wanted to be better than a slave to a feudal economic system. He proposed to her and she accepted, although her family were beside themselves with anger and disappointment. Bob's reputation had influenced them if it had not her.

CHAPTER FOUR

A BARBER AND HIS FIDDLE

On August 15, 1926 Bob married. He had only his good intentions to offer a wife. He took her with him that fall pulling bolls in other men's fields to earn their eating money. As he worked he wondered why he had done this thing. Why should he have thought he could support and take care of another person when up to now it had been more than he could do to take care of himself? He decided it would be best to go back to Amarillo in search of work. If he found anything this time he would stick to it. He would not be as fickle to his masters as he had been before.

A few days before Christmas he was working in a field making his plans when his father drove up. "What on earth are you doin' here, poppa?" he exclaimed. "It's 150 miles from home. Is somebody bad sick?"

"Don't you remember, Jim? We got to play the ranch dance. It's Christmas time."

When Bob's reputation as a fiddler had first spread, a cowboy was sent to him from a ranch a county or so away to find out if he were a member of the Wills family in east Texas. The rancher's wife had known Johnnie and his family when she was a child but had not known that he was living in west Texas now. She had heard of Jim Rob Wills as a fiddler and if he were any relation she wanted him to play for a Christmas dance at her ranch house. Bob and his father had both gone much to her delight. She told them that she would expect them to come every year. The Christmas before Johnnie showed up in the field, Bob had played the dance alone. He stood in a doorway playing for two rooms of dancers. By one o'clock in the morning the hair of his bow wore out, he played so hard. He played for five hours more with just the stick and managed to play danceable music.

Johnnie was so eager for Bob to come that he could not refuse. Four rooms of the ranch house had been thrown open for the dancing. There were 200 people there and the rancher's wife had hired some other musicians to play for one room, expecting Bob and his father to keep the remaining three rooms dancing.

The Wills' music was so superior that only a couple or two would dance in the last room. The ignored musicians were angry and wondered if they would be paid well since no one would dance to their music. Bob felt sorry for them and during an intermission talked to them in a friendly way. When they offered him a drink he accepted. A little later he keeled over and his father had to take him away. The drink had been doped. It was three days before he came to his senses.

Such jealous double dealing disgusted him. He did not want to touch a fiddle again. Fiddling had always been a joy to him. He entertained people for the pleasure it gave him. If it were going to mix him up in affairs like that, then he was through. It was with relief that he left for Amarillo.

Since he had the ability of making friends and entertaining people, he thought he might make a good salesman. An insurance company hired him and he was soon disillusioned. He could sell himself to a dance crowd, but he could not sell one person anything. He tried cars, but gave up after he had given a customer the best sales talk of which he was capable and the man still refused. "Would you take this car if I'd give it to you?" Bob asked. "Well, I don't know," the man parried. "That's what I thought," Bob said and ended his career as a salesman.

He helped survey a telephone line from Amarillo to Border. He kept a rooming house. He did carpenter work. He was a common laborer. He could settle at none of these occupations. After six months he gave up and decided once more to go back to the land. He had saved some money and bought a small farm near his father's, complete with team and implements.

As he worked with his first crop the idea began to formulate that perhaps his fiddling was the one important thing that he could do. That vague idea that someday he might have a band if he could go to school first came back to him again. This time he did not stifle it. Of course he would have to study music as he could not read a note and knew nothing about musical arrangements. The only thing he could do was play a fiddle better than most people are ever privileged to hear one played, and keep an audience constantly entertained. Since nothing he did seemed to satisfy him or claim his complete interest except fiddle playing why not work to accomplish that vague hope? Why not plan to study music?

He looked at his gloved hands resting on the plough. He had stood a lot of teasing about those hands. He always wore gloves when doing farm work, for he did not want his hands to become thick and calloused with labor. It would spoil his fiddle playing. The men made good-humored fun of his soft, white hands, but Bob ignored their thrusts. When he had done carpenter work and smashed a finger while driving a nail, he had suffered more mentally than physically, wondering if it would hurt his finger so he could not use it again. In spite of his care, his hands showed wear and the palms were not as smooth as he would have liked. That was the trouble with farm work—in a few more years his hands would be gnarled. It was not the only trouble either. How could he save enough money to take music lessons when it was hard enough to get money just to live? It was all so complicated. His story would be like Johnnie's—a feudal slave to the farm.

As he studied his hands, he thought that if he were a barber he could keep them as they should be kept. A barber was always working with lotions and soap and water. He did not do anything that would hurt his hands. A barber made money, too, didn't he? Well, why couldn't he take up barbering? It would keep his hands tender and he could save money for his music lessons.

No sooner did he complete his first crop than he sold the farm. Johnnie shook his head over his eldest son. He told him how foolish he was and that nobody with sense would act like he did, always going away and coming back and never settling down to anything.

Bob's wife stuck quietly by him. Anything he wanted to do was all right with her. She preferred to keep in the background. Just to be near him was enough. It did not matter where they went.

After he had enrolled in a barber college in Amarillo and set aside enough money for living expenses there was a little left over with which he could begin his music lessons. The few that he took were disappointing. He could play so much better than his teacher that it was hard to listen respectfully to criticism. His mind stubbornly refused to interest itself in the whys and wherefores of the little black notes. His ear could learn a tune in less time than the most skillful juggler of symbols could commit it. Barbering was much easier. He could shave a bottle with fine gestures and completed his course and received his diploma in half the time that most students took.

Although he successfully passed his state examinations and had a fancy scrolled orange and white certificate with an impressive gold seal stating that he was a legal barber, he was doubtful as to whether he could yet satisfy high class people with his work. Maybe he should practice on Mexicans first.

It was the end of 1927 when he arrived in Roy, New Mexico, with his wife, his certificate and his barber tools. He figured that the Mexican population of that little town would provide enough material for him. His frank desire to cater to Mexicans made the other people slightly suspicious of him. They thought perhaps he had killed a man by a slip of the razor and did not trust himself any longer.

He leased a corner of a pool hall and set up shop. The Mexicans came, all right, and soon the other people, for his prices were reasonable, his work was good and they liked him.

One afternoon a good looking, young Mexican girl with a long mane of glossy, black hair sat down in the barber chair and said, "Hair cut."

"How short?" Bob asked. She mumbled something which he took to be "short." Thinking she did not speak English very well, he questioned her no further and began work. He decided that if she wanted a short hair cut she would get it. She probably could not afford more than one hair cut a year anyway and would like to have it last. He had a fine time snipping away. When he was finished, her hair was off almost to the top of her ears.

He handed her a mirror. She took one look and yelled. He had no doubt as to how well she could speak English then, for she cursed him in as fluent a stream of colloquial language as the staring pool room habitues could have managed. The mumbling which he mistook for "short" had in actuality been "not very short."

She flounced out of the shop leaving him chagrined and the butt of pool room laughter.

A BARBER AND HIS FIDDLE

That night he played at a Mexican dance. The girl was present and was the only one with a hat on. She glared angrily at him throughout the evening.

A month or so later Bob offered free neck shaves as a specialty to induce more customers. The same girl came in and demanded one.

"If I give you a neck shave, will you let me cut your hair when you get ready to have it cut?" he demanded.

"But look what you did before," she protested.

"That don't make no difference. I'll cut your hair just like you want it and do the best hair cuttin' job you ever got. But I ain't goin' to give you no free neck shave unless you promise to come back."

The girl promised.

"I'll break this neck of yours if you go to any other barber," Bob said sternly as he dusted it off following the shave. The girl grinned. When her hair needed cutting she was back. Bob had made a customer of her in spite of his mistake.

After he had gained his experience he was eager to leave, for the town offered no future possibilities. The trouble was that it did not even offer enough possibilities for him to earn the money necessary to leave. He was puzzling over his next move when he made the acquaintance of an itinerant watch tinker. Like Bob he had no money and wanted to leave.

While discussing their situation they ran across an old sample book of suit materials. They looked them over and conceived the idea of selling some suits to members of a construction gang working on a highway just outside of Roy. One evening they went to the camp and did a persuasive selling job procuring a number of orders. Although neither of them knew anything about taking proper measurements, they solemnly and with great show measured the men by lamp light. They made such an impression that they were invited to stay for dinner. The men were delighted to buy clothes at what they considered a good bargain.

Bob and the tinker sent in the orders, pocketed the profits and left town. Some years later Bob discovered that it was fortunate they had not waited for the suits to arrive or they would have been forced to file a few assault and battery charges. The lamp light and their inexperience resulted in the sleeves of some suits reaching three inches below the hands, trousers too short and general misfits.

He left his wife and a $12 grocery bill in Roy, promising to send money for them both as soon as possible. For five weeks he free lanced as a barber in Lakeview and other towns where he was known. In Turkey he landed a job in the best barber shop, taking the fourth chair back. He had enough money to take care of the grocery bill and get his wife before going to work, so he drove back in an old, borrowed car.

On the return trip to Turkey the chances of his having a career as either a barber or a fiddler narrowed to a minimum for one hectic night. The car, which was past the age of caring whether it went or not, stalled in the middle of a river they were fording. The river was rising, so they abandoned the car in order to get to shore before the water got to them. They were taken in for the night by some hospitable but destitute squatters who invited them to share the dirt floor of their shack for a night's rest. Awakening in the morning stiff with discomfort they were horrified to see several rattlesnakes coiled comfortably in the room with them. The squatters beat them away in an unconcerned fashion, commenting that the snakes sought shelter with them during the rainy season. Bob had killed many a rattlesnake in the fields, but having them as bedfellows made him feel a little weak inside.

Bob was a popular barber in Turkey, for he kept his fiddle in the shop. During the slack hours he would entertain the loafers and customers with a tune or two. He was not in such good standing with the shop owner for too many requests came for him to play during busy hours and he did not attend to the work as much as was expected. For example, one Saturday night somebody ran into the shop and called to Bob that a fiddling contest was being held down the street. Bob grabbed his fiddle, joined the contestants, played one tune, received the first prize of $5 and went back to his barbering.

He soon found out that barbering and fiddling were clashing rather than abetting each other, as he had originally planned. Saturday nights were the times when everyone wanted him to play for dances. They were also the times when everyone came to town to be barbered. Somehow he managed to do both, although barbering suffered.

He was not making money and was continually in debt. At one time he was so far behind on his furniture and grocery bill that he had to make some money quick. He hired an abandoned garage for $10 on the cuff and had some handbills announcing a dance for the next Saturday night made on the same arrangement. His friends helped him distribute them in the surrounding towns. Then he asked a piano player and a guitarist to play with him, promising them a percentage of the profits. The young guitarist said he would play for $5 but he wanted his money in advance. Bob was exasperated, but borrowed the money from one of the other barbers and paid him.

The garage was jammed the night of the dance. They took in $240 at the gate. Bob's personal share was $190 and the young guitarist was a sick color because of his short sightedness. Bob felt sorry for him and slipped him a few dollars extra which only made him feel worse, thinking of the great number of extras he might have had.

This absurdly easy way of raising money did not encourage Bob to start a band then and there and give up barbering for good. It was a stunt that could only be repeated occasionally, for it was farming country and dances could be held only on Saturday nights during the good seasons, which were short. A constant supply of cash is a rarity with a farmer. The musicians that worked with Bob were not really musicians. They were kids who worked on the farm and played as a recreation. They did not play particularly well and they would not have had the time to do the regular rehearsing which a band requires. Besides, he would have lost face with his friends and the cash customers if he had turned to the fiddle as a business. If you did not do good, hard, physical labor you were considered "no account" and were relegated to the lowest standing in the community. That having a band and playing an instrument was hard work was something that no one could have understood or accepted as the truth. They did not know anything about it.

Toward the end of the year when everyone was in the fields and both barbering and fiddling were slow to create business, Bob bought a few patches of cotton and made a small profit.

This was the sort of existence that Bob led during 1928 and 1929. Although there was no excess money in his pockets, his fiddling was improving steadily. His self-confidence had been healed. His popularity was greater among his own people than it had ever been before. As for the future—well, it would take care of itself. Right now, he was enjoying living.

Toward the end of 1929 a medicine show came to Turkey. It was not as well received as it rightly expected to be, for the crowds booed its fiddler. "We've got a fellow right here with us who can out-fiddle your man," they told the owner time and again. "Our fiddler is the best one in the country."

The annoyed owner demanded to hear this local prodigy and Bob consented to play. The medicine show group was forced to admit that the customers were right. Quick to take advantage of such a popular find, the owner offered Bob a job to fiddle and play black face. Bob was just as quick to accept. Here was a chance to crash the entertainment world without a long period of study. It was just a small, cheap show, but there was a great deal of glamour about it for him. Like the rest of the country people he believed the tall tales and fantasies that the show people manufactured as part of their business. Bob had dreams of plenty of money, fame and a glittering future.

Two weeks on the road with them deflated the air castles he had blown up so innocently. After working with the men he became aware of their shoddiness. They were not his kind of people. His dislike spoiled his performances and the owner told him to leave.

His inglorious return to Turkey rankled in his heart. His friends were superior. "Well, you're back just as I thought, because I knew that about two weeks was all you would last," was the refrain he heard everywhere. The old feeling of failure sprang up at this encouragement. He had quit the barber shop airily and when he humbly asked for his job back, he was told just as airily that it was not available. However, the owner said in a condescending way, he could take an old chair in the back of the shop and pick up what business he could.

Bob was dissatisfied and unhappy with this offer. The little taste of medicine show life had spoiled him for every day routine. Yet, it did not occur to him to leave or to find something else to do.

CHAPTER FIVE

IRON BARS FREE A PRISONER

Then came the turning point in his entire career. Bob is thankful now that what happened did happen, but at the time, and for many months afterwards, he was humiliated whenever he thought about it.

The Sunday following his crestfallen return from the traveling show, his unhappiness was sharper than ever. He started drinking with several of his young friends. He began to feel better. By the time the bunch had driven to Lakeview for a ball game he was hilarious. The excitement of the game added to more liquor completed the job. At sundown the boys drove into Turkey thoroughly drunk.

They parked in front of the drug store and Bob was left in the rumbleseat while the others went in for some cigars. Several women parked beside him and Bob, still in the baseball mood, began to yell and laugh. The town law later said that the women asked that Bob be put away, but whatever the reason, he asked Bob to come along with him. As Bob had been on many a party with the law, he thought that this was just a continuation of his good time and staggered down the street with him.

He did not notice where they were going as he did not care. Anything for a good time! When the law opened a door, Bob walked in, but when he heard the door lock behind him, he sobered up. He was in the town calaboose—a tiny, stiflingly hot, one-room affair with a single, barred window.

For a little while he yelled and pounded with rage, but he was there for the night. He disdained the cot that the room offered, so, spreading his handkerchief on the cement floor for a pillow, he went to sleep.

In the meantime, his friends had discovered his absence. When they found out where he was, they were more infuriated than he. The two laws saw that the situation was more than they could handle, so, instead of arresting Bob's companions in drunkenness, they solved the problem by leaving town.

Hubbin' It

The next morning Bob awakened to find that his brand new $56 suit and $10 shoes had suffered more than he had from the mishaps of the previous day and night. This did not make him feel any better. His anger began to mount as the morning wore on and nobody came to let him out. The laws had not forgotten that Jim Rob Wills had spent the night in the calaboose. They were uncomfortably aware of the fact that he was still there. As a matter of fact, they were arguing about who was going to let him out. Jim Rob was too popular in the town and he was too willing to physically right what he considered a personal offense. Neither one of them cared to be the one to face him on this the morning after, when Jim Rob was sober.

"You let him out," one of them argued. "You're the one who put him in. I didn't."

"Yeah, but I'm off duty now," was the answer. "It's your job."

It was late when one of them gave in. He came around to the window first and called to Bob. He apologized and wanted to make sure that there were no hard feelings. Bob had little to say, and the law had less as they walked up the alley to the main street.

There was a head stuck out of every shop in town curious to see what was going to happen. Aware of his audience and feeling a vague stirring of duty, the law spoke in a loud voice, "Now, Jim Rob, you'd better lay off the whiskey from now on."

Bob's anger broke. "Listen you," he yelled. "You don't need to tell me that when you've probably got a hangover yourself now. I was the only one you put in jail, when everybody else in this town gets drunk. The trouble isn't my drinkin' whiskey. The trouble is that this town is too small and everybody in it is too small."

Bob stalked into the barber shop and picked up his tools.

"What's the matter, Jim Rob?" the owner asked.

"I'm leavin' town and I'm never comin' back here to live. You're drivin' all the good people out of town and I hate to say what kind of people are left. You'll find out you've made a mistake."

Bob walked firmly down the street and out of town as a fascinated audience composed of almost the entire population silently watched him go. A few of the young boys drove up to him in their cars and offered him a lift. But Bob held his place in the middle of the road and told them to get away from him.

As the road lengthened between him and Turkey his ties to the kind of life he had always led began to break. He was disgusted. He was angry. Although he was unaware of it, he was finally free. There were to be many agonizing times when he would be broke and hungry, when he would falter, and when fate would seem to be trying to kick him back. But he was destined to go up now.

In 1936 he was to come back to Turkey with as much triumph as he had left with disgrace. He was to play a dance to which the entire town would turn out and everybody would be eager to shake his hand and congratulate him. He would be the hero of every small boy in Turkey and the pride of every adult citizen. His name was to become one of Turkey's chief claims to fame and he was to feel grateful for and be proud of his friendships there. But now he felt that the town had humiliated him and he was bitter. However, he was already in Turkey's debt, for he resolved, as he angrily sculled a rock or two out of his way, to stop drinking—a resolution which he kept.

CHAPTER SIX

BLACK FACE AND BLACK TIMES

Bob had no plans. He did not know where he wanted to go or what he would do when he got there. He finally decided that Dallas would be as likely a place as any. He knew that even if he could not do anything with his fiddling, he could at least eat by barbering.

By alternately catching rides and walking he came to a little town some sixty miles from Turkey. Out of funds, he looked for a job. He found one in a barber shop and early on a Saturday morning began working. By one o'clock Sunday morning he was shaving his last customer without enthusiasm, for the long day's profits were less than $8.

The old man in his barber chair was not a stranger to Bob. He was the owner of a large second hand store. Bob had seen a fiddle in its window and asked if he might play it. The old man had been pleased with his playing.

"Do you know anybody who would like to drive me to Ft. Worth in my car?" the second hand store man asked another barber in the shop.

Bob offered to do it, so it was arranged that they would meet at a filling station in three hours.

It was not as lucky a break as Bob thought at first. The old man let him spend his $8 for gasoline and breakfast and did not offer to reimburse him. Bob was too proud to ask him for it. When the old man dropped him in front of a cheap hotel in Ft. Worth, he had just enough change left to pay for his bed for the night.

The next day Bob looked for a barbering job, but Ft. Worth was full of jobless barbers. He ran into one from a little town near his own and this fellow let Bob stay with him a few nights although he only had $3 himself.

In the meantime the second hand store man had looked Bob up and asked him to accompany him on his rounds of the pawnshops to advise him on good fiddle bargains. Bob helped him pick out fifty fiddles. When the work was all done, Bob asked if he might buy one of the fiddles on credit. He said he would see that the money was paid within three months regardless of what happened. He fully expected that the old man would give him a fiddle out of gratitude for his help. But, no, the fellow said he would not trust him.

"Old man," Bob said. "I've always held old age in respect, but your age don't make me respect you now. You are the meanest, the most good for nothin' old man I ever met. I wouldn't take one of your fiddles if you give it to me. Someday you'll be sorry you turned me down. You're the kind of man that's never been worth nothin' to nobody, you ain't now and you never will be!"

The old man had nothing to say.

About eight years later, Bob happened to be driving through the old man's town and while his car was being serviced he walked into the second hand shop. He was curious to see if the old man was still living. He was. "I'm the boy you wouldn't let buy a fiddle on credit," Bob told him. "I've made enough money fiddlin' now so's I could buy your shop if I wanted to." The only answer the old man had was to ask Bob if he would give him an opinion on a fiddle which he had and thought was valuable. Bob refused to look at the fiddle and left saying, "I don't know how much that fiddle is worth, but I do know that whatever it's worth you'll get your money out of it and more."

However, it was a discouraged Bob Wills who left the old man that day in 1929, unable to buy a fiddle, no money, not even the possibility of finding a barber job, which he had thought would be his meal ticket.

Then he thought of the medicine shows. Whenever he had talked to medicine show men on the road they had told him that any time he wanted a job to come see them at headquarters in Ft. Worth. As medicine show men make their living according to how agile their tongues and imaginations are, they had built up quite a picture in the country boy's mind, in spite of his one disillusioning experience. He thought that they must live in fine homes in Ft. Worth and that the laboratories where the medicines were mixed were big factories with doctors in white coats attending to details, while shiny machines did the manufacturing.

Hubbin' It

With this glowing picture in mind he called Gassoway, the head of all the shows. Gassoway gave him the address of the headquarters and asked him to come over.

When Bob walked into a dirty two room shack he thought he must be in the wrong place. But there was Gassoway with an unshaven face and soiled clothes. An enormous, ugly woman was pouring "medicine" into bottles. Bob came to earth with a thud. He saw immediately what medicine show business was—nothing but talk. But he had to have a job. He had to eat. Gassoway could not place him in any of his units, but he mentioned a "Doc" who was organizing a show.

Bob called Doc, who gave him an address five miles away and told him he would look him over if he came out. As he had no bus fare, Bob trudged to his home, managing to add two extra miles due to a wrong turn. He was hungry and tired when he arrived.

Doc, a fat, heavy-jowled man in his late fifties with a blustery air, opened the door waving a shaving brush in one hand. He continued his shaving while he interviewed Bob.

"Can you sing?" he asked gruffly.

"Yes, sir."

"Well, let's hear you. Sing a song."

"I ain't got any music and it's hard to sing right off hand."

"I thought you said you could sing."

"Yes sir, I can, but . . ." Bob was growing angry. Doc was being unreasonable.

"All right, if you can't sing, can you dance?"

"Yes, sir, a little."

"Roll up the rug and let's see you."

Bob protested again. Mrs. Doc, a pretty young woman, who had been listening to the conversation from the kitchen, intervened for him and told her husband he was not being fair. After discussing Bob's other qualifications, Doc said he would hire him, but that the show would not be organized for another ten days. However, a platform had to be built on a truck and other jobs done first. If Bob wanted to join he could start work now and Doc would see that he

Privately printed, the original 1938 edition of *Hubbin' It* was available
only through mail order. In addition to the book, one received this
photo of Bob, detached and suitable for framing.
(Courtesy of Bob Pinson)

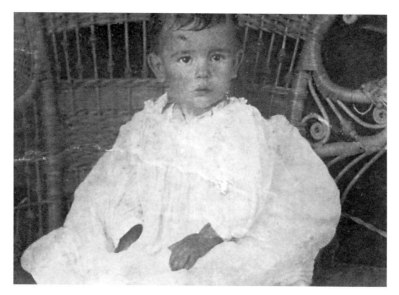

Bob at eight months.

Emma and Johnnie with their year-old son, Bob.

Picking cotton with a little cousin in 1926.

A two dollar fiddle in 1923.

A sixteen hundred dollar fiddle in 1938.

During "preaching" days in Knox County at the age of 17.

Bob and his father at Memphis, Texas, in 1915.

Bob Wills and His Texas Playboys.
Left to right: Everett Stover, trumpet; Leon McAuliffe, steel guitar; Charles Laughton, saxophone; O. W. Mayo, business manager; Robert "Zeb" McNally, saxophone; Herman Arnspiger, guitar; Bob Wills, guitar; William Eschol "Smokey" Dacus, drummer; Tommy Duncan, singer; Clifton "Sleepy" Johnson, fiddle; Johnnie Lee Wills, banjo; Jesse Ashlock, fiddle; Joe Ferguson, bass fiddle; Al Stricklin, piano; Eldon Shamblin, guitar.

The Texas Playboys in 1935, in front of their touring tri-motor Stinson. From the left: Johnnie Lee Wills, Smokey Dacus, Bob Wills, Tommy Duncan, Jesse Ashlock, Son Lansford, Sleepy Johnson, pilot Earl Fields, Leon McAuliffe, Zeb McNally, Art Haines.

Top: Bob and the band in front of Cain's Dancing Academy, Tulsa, Oklahoma, 1934.
Center: Keeping the dance floor filled on a Saturday night in Tulsa.
Bottom: In September 1935, Wills and the Texas Playboys, not yet settled into their Western motif, borrowed these uniforms from the Cities Service Oil Company.
(Photos courtesy of Glenn White)

Top: The Texas Playboys in front of the sedan they
jokingly said they "pushed" to Oklahoma.
Center: After one month on the air in Tulsa, Bob Wills
had already received this small mountain of fan mail.
Bottom: Bob shares the spotlight with Gene Autry for
a live broadcast from a hotel in Texarkana, Texas, 1937.
(Photos courtesy of Glenn White)

Ready to swing in 1934. Left to right: Manager O. W. Mayo, Art Haines, Zeb McNally, Leon McAuliffe, Herman Arnspiger, Sleepy Johnson, Bob Wills, Smokey Dacus, Jesse Ashlock, Johnnie Lee Wills, Tommy Duncan, Son Lansford.

Top: Conducting the boys in 1934. Left to right: Bob Wills, Art Haines, Uncle John Wills (seated), Zeb McNally, Jesse Ashlock, Sleepy Johnson, Leon McAuliffe, Smokey Dacus, Johnnie Lee Wills, Herman Arnspiger Son Lansford, Tommy Duncan, O. W. Mayo.

Bottom: Cutting up with the boys in 1936. Standing, left to right: Ray DeGeer, Everett Stover, Zeb McNally, Bob Wills, Johnnie Lee Wills, O. W. Mayo, Al Stricklin, Tommy Duncan, Leon McAuliffe, Sleepy Johnson. Foreground: Smokey Dacus, Jesse Ashlock, Herman Arnspiger, Joe Ferguson.

BOB WILLS AND HIS TEXAS PLAYBOYS ⬤ OKeh Records
See other side for list of releases.

HEAR THESE LATEST HITS BY

★ BOB WILLS ★

and his

TEXAS PLAYBOYS

06371 LIL LIZA JANE BOB WILLS STOMP	**05523** MEDLEY OF SPANISH WALTZES BLUE BONNET RAG
06327 LYLA LOU TWIN GUITAR SPECIAL	**05401** PRAY FOR THE LIGHTS TO GO OUT
06205 MAIDEN'S PRAYER TAKIN' IT HOME	TWINKLE TWINKLE LITTLE STAR
06101 NEW WORRIED MIND TAKE ME BACK TO TULSA	**05333** SOPHISTICATED HULA BLUE PRELUDE
05905 BIG BEAVER THERE'S GOING TO BE A PARTY	**05282** DRUNKARD BLUES DON'T LET THE DEAL GO DOWN
05753 THAT BROWNSKIN GAL TIME CHANGES EVERY- THING	**05228** PROSPERITY SPECIAL IF I COULD BRING BACK MY BUDDY
05694 NEW SAN ANTONIO ROSE BOB WILLS' SPECIAL	**05161** MY WINDOW FACES THE SOUTH
05637 LONE STAR RAG I DON'T LOV'A NOBODY	DREAMY EYES WALTZ
05597 YOU DON'T LOVE ME NO WONDER	**05079** IDA RED CAROLINA IN THE MORNING

35¢ OKEH RECORDS OKeh

Postcard-sized promotional material plugging Wills's records, circa 1941.

The Texas Playboys posed behind a fair display for Play Boy Flour in Enid, Oklahoma, 1936. The rider on the flour sacks is Tommy Duncan.

got his meals and a place to sleep until the show opened. That meant no salary, but Bob, thinking of no food or bed that night if he did not accept, was ready to take any offer.

For the next ten days he slept on a pallet in Doc's kitchen and worked with two young fellows, Jim and Richard, building the truck platform and performing the other necessary jobs.

Jim could play the banjo fairly well and Richard could just equal his ability on the guitar. Bob listened to them and decided that they would make a pleasing enough background for his fiddle.

One afternoon he went to radio station WBAP and asked to see the manager. The little receptionist was very friendly to him and finally managed the interview.

"What do you want?" the manager asked sharply. Bob's ragged clothes did not make an impressive appearance.

"Do you ever use a fiddle band on your programs?" Bob asked.

"What have you got to offer?"

"Well, I just play the fiddle."

"What kind of a band do you have with you?"

"No kind."

"Where's your fiddle?"

"I ain't got one."

"Well, what on earth ... what kind of a place do you think this is, to come in here without anything and try to get a job? You must be crazy. I can't waste time with you now. If you would come with a band and a fiddle I might listen to you, but I never heard of such a thing!"

"That's all I wanted to know. I just wondered if you would be interested in that kind of music. I'll come back with it!"

Leaving the manager to his annoyance, Bob went back to Doc and borrowed $1.50 to buy a $2.50 fiddle he had noticed and liked in a pawnshop. The owner trusted him for the other dollar. Taking Jim and Richard in tow, he was back at the station within two days. Jim had his banjo in a flour sack and was swinging it gaily along. Richard had his guitar slung over his shoulder by a frayed string. Bob realized what an unfavorable appearance the group made in their cheap, worn clothes. He did the best he could on such short notice. "Jim, you throw that flour sack away," he said angrily. "What will they think of us? Quit swinging it. Hold it up close to you and walk along decent. Richard, take that string off that guitar. Don't you two snigger when we get in there. Try and act like you got some brain cells."

Properly chastened, the two did as they were told and followed him into the station. It was still a seedy looking trio of young men that asked the receptionist if they could see the manager. Some musicians lounging in the hall did not bother to stifle their guffaws when they looked at Bob and the boys. Bob's heart sank, but the girl, feeling sorry for them, saw to it that they got an audition immediately.

They had played only half a tune, with the musicians laughing at them through the studio glass, when the manager came storming into the room.

"Boys, you're good! Can you go on the air right away?" A bit bewildered, they nodded. The station cut a broadcast of records short and put them on the air for half an hour.

Quite a few fan letters were received for that brief program. Fiddle music was new to the radio. However, the manager did not have a sponsor for them and refused to pay them himself. He wanted them to play every Sunday night. His theory was, "It's a fifty-fifty proposition. I supply the power. You supply the music." Bob did not like the idea. He could play his fiddle free anywhere. It was money he wanted, not applause. As the medicine show was ready to open, they broke their relationship with the studio after playing several broadcasts.

The day before the show was to open in Riverside, a suburb of the city, he asked Doc when the show people would arrive and when they would rehearse for the performance.

"Why, Jim and Richard and you and me, we're the show," Doc replied.

Bob was horrified. "What kind of a show do you think you can put on with us ?"

"We'll put black on old Jim there," Doc explained. "He'll look funny and we'll put chin whiskers on old Richard and they can play the banjo and guitar a little, and you can fiddle and I'll talk."

BLACK FACE AND BLACK TIMES

"Doc, if that's the kind of show you're set on puttin' on, you can do it. But you open without me. I ain't appearin' with them. I thought you knew show business, but you'll get rotten egged out of Riverside if you try to do that."

Doc argued that he had to open the show because he had advertised it for a week. Bob was firm. He said that the only condition upon which he would appear with them would be that they go to Riverside, play one or two tunes, and announce that due to hard luck some of the players had not arrived and that the show would open two nights later. When Mrs. Doc agreed with Bob, the old show man gave in and followed Bob's plan.

Then the group assembled to plan the acts. A few of Mrs. Doc's relatives and friends acted as an audience and at Bob's request Doc presented his ideas of what the entertainment should be. It was a pitiful attempt. The trial audience was painfully silent.

When Bob figured Doc was genuinely discouraged he asked if he were ready to listen to some suggestions. Doc was.

"I'll put on black face and we'll work out an act with Mrs. Doc as the leading lady and you as her husband. Let Jim and Richard act natural and they'll be funny enough, but don't let them try to be funny or they'll make you cry."

Mrs. Doc protested that she did not want to be on the stage, but when Bob asked her if she wanted them to make money to live on, she agreed. They rehearsed all that day and the next.

When the show opened it was a hit. The audience yelled for more and showed its appreciation by buying $366 worth of medicine and candy.

Bob was the star of the show. Not only did the performance attract the usual medicine show audience, but wealthy people would stop their cars to see what was going on and stay until the end. Many of them came back to see Bob and asked him why he was wasting his talent on a cheap medicine show when he should be in a downtown theater.

The question of salary arose. Doc had told Bob before the show opened that he would pay him $10 a week. After the third tremendously successful performance Bob said he believed he deserved a raise. "Oh, yes, I've already raised you to $12.50 a week," Doc said quickly.

HUBBIN' IT

Bob was silent until the end of the first week and then told Doc that it was ridiculous to expect him to continue at such a low salary. He demanded $35 a week. Doc said that was impossible. Bob walked out. He did not even return to Doc's house for his clothes, but having located a distant uncle living in town, went to his house to spend the night.

The show flopped without Bob that night. Within a few minutes the crowd was yelling, "We want Rastus! We want Rastus!" Doc was forced to close. The next morning he was searching for Bob. It was not long before he found him, as Bob had asked Mrs. Doc's sister to get his clothes for him. He had no desire to see Doc again. When Doc heard where he was waiting, he drove over and persuaded him to get in the car. Arguing all the way, he took him back to his home. Doc was now willing to pay $15. The answer was no.

Bob collected his belongings and was ready to depart. Doc used every pretext to detain him and finally asked him to shave him before he left. Bob agreed, for he had thought of a plan.

He put in a collect telephone call for Cross-eyed Wilson, a medicine show man whom he knew was in San Saba at the moment. While he was waiting for the operator to locate Wilson he began to shave Doc. He was half finished when Wilson was on the wire. Wilson had no idea who Jim Rob Wills was, but he had accepted the call fearing it might be of importance to him.

"Mr. Wilson, this is Jim Rob Wills, that fiddler you were looking for," Bob said. ("I don't want any fiddler and I never heard of you," Wilson sputtered.)

"Oh, you want me to come right away?" ("Don't you dare come down here!")

"Forty dollars a week? That'll be fine, Mr. Wilson." ("What's this all about? Are you drunk? I wouldn't pay no fiddler forty *cents* a week even!")

The half-shaven Doc was hanging on Bob's shoulder. "Don't accept, Bob, don't accept," he was whispering urgently. "Tell him you'll call him back."

"And you'll pay my transportation down there? Why, that sure is nice of you, Mr. Wilson. But there's something else going on here and I'll let you know later whether I'll be there or not." ("Get off this phone! It's costing me money! You'd better not show up down here or you won't live no longer!" Wilson was cursing with rage as he hung up.)

BLACK FACE AND BLACK TIMES

Doc begged Bob not to take the "offer," but to stay and he would give him $20 a week. Bob, acting thoroughly disgusted, walked out of the house and started down the road. He had no prospect of a job anywhere, but he was determined to carry the bluff out until he obtained what he wanted or nothing.

Doc yelled that he would give him $25 a week.

"Listen, Doc, you don't need to call me again—even if you'd offer me $34.99 I wouldn't take it. Why should I work for you for that when I can get me a job for $40?" Bob walked on.

Doc puffed down the road after him. "All right, Bob, if you want to take all the profits of the show and not leave nothin' for nobody else, you can have it," he conceded sourly.

"If that's the way you are goin' to feel about it, I wouldn't work for you at all!" Bob turned away again.

"Oh, all right, Bob. The show ain't no good without you and if I don't get you to come back my wife'll quit me, she's so mad about the whole thing. I'm sorry."

Bob's bluff had worked. He was with the show for the next six months. But when it broke up for the winter he was the loser after all. He had only taken enough money each week to pay expenses. Doc said he would keep the balance for him. When Bob asked for the balance, Doc did not have it. He had borrowed it to pay back his own debts.

Chapter Seven

A Taste of Fame Turns Sour

The medicine show toured as long into the winter as possible. During the last few weeks, it was so cold that Bob had to play his fiddle with gloves on and the old people who came to watch the performances brought hot bricks to keep their feet warm. Not only was it a piercingly cold winter, but it was the bleak winter of 1930, when the depression took its greatest toll from the cotton country.

The group disbanded in Alvarado, where they had played for three weeks and Bob had been a great personal hit. He decided that he would stay there and go back to barbering. His popularity as a black face should have brought him customers to the barber shop where he managed to find a job. But, unfortunately, Bob was such a good showman that no one knew him without his black make-up. Frequently the customer he was shaving would praise the ability of the black face who had left town. The other barbers would not tell the customers that this was the comedian they liked so well, as they were not eager for all the trade to go Bob's way. Bob was too proud to tell them himself. So business was not as good as he had anticipated.

At Christmas time his father came through with some friends and talked Bob into going to east Texas with him. Once there, Bob was sorry he had consented, for it was "fiddle, fiddle, fiddle" every minute. He had to sneak out of town away from his friends and relatives in order to get any sleep.

His father wanted him to come back to the farm, but Bob could see no advantage in such a move. There was no money there. His father could not borrow much. There was no work to be done. On the other hand, Bob did not know where else he could go. His wife and year-old baby girl were with him which made the situation more acute. They had been staying first with his family and then with hers for the past year.

A Taste Of Fame Turns Sour

Headed for he knew not where, Bob and his family stopped overnight in Ft. Worth. That night another turning point in his career came—this time in the shape of Herman Arnspiger, a young guitar player. While Bob was playing the medicine show he had become acquainted with Herman, who admired him and his fiddle playing. Herman had a job three nights a week in a cotton mill. The other nights he would join the show in whatever nearby town it was pitched and add his guitar music to the program. Bob discovered that Herman's guitar playing blended more pleasingly with his fiddle than that of anyone with whom he had ever played.

It was chance that they met that night. Herman had lost his job and like Bob was wondering what to do next. After talking to him, Bob decided that he would stay in Ft. Worth. It was just possible the two of them might find something to do at one of the radio stations.

Whenever Bob makes a decision, he immediately starts to work to put it over, which is one of the most important reasons why he has been able to get ahead. Many people would call the things that happen to him luck, but they are really the result of determination and nerve.

It was a sorry looking couple of poorly dressed young men who wandered into radio station KTAT holding a fiddle and a guitar. As they stood uncertainly in the reception hall, they were accosted by a fellow asking what they wanted. This fellow happened to be the leader of a fiddle band that played a commercial program for a chicken hatchery twice a week.

"I'm a fiddler and I'm lookin' for a job," Bob said.

"You're wasting your time here," the fellow replied. "They don't need any fiddlers. Our band takes care of that for them. You might as well go along."

Tiny Stowe, the station manager, was standing nearby unnoticed and overheard the conversation.

"I don't know about that," he said, stepping forward. "Your sponsors have been complaining about you. If these two fellows are any good it just may be that there is a need for them. Come along, boys, let me hear you."

He was so delighted with the music of Bob and Herman that he hired them immediately to take over the chicken hatchery program.

The few dollars a week they earned in this way was not enough.

HUBBIN' IT

Although it was against station rules to work for any other station, they managed to obtain a program at KFJZ and another at WBAP. All three stations were pleased with them thinking that they had them exclusively.

The manager of KTAT was so proud of his "discovery" that he made a standing offer of $50 to anyone who was a better fiddler than Bob Wills. One day he heard Bob's program over one of the other stations. When Bob arrived later he called him into his office.

"Bob, I heard a fiddle player this afternoon that was good," he said in a worried tone. "I don't say he was better than you are, but he was just as good. You'd better not let me lose that $50."

Bob smiled and was silent. He was secretly worried. No one knew that he was competing with himself, but if the stations found out he was working for them all, he was likely to be out of a job all the way around.

As the spring changed into summer some of the programs were discontinued. Although they still had a few small programs, Bob and Herman decided to make the medicine shows. They also played country dances wherever they could find an engagement.

One night at a country dance just outside of Ft. Worth the crowd was responding nicely to their music and everybody was having a good time when a young man walked in. He was dressed in a flashy, prosperous fashion and his appearance made him stand out from among the farmers like a rose in a bunch of cacti. He was accompanied by two other young men. "Here come a bunch of smart alecs," Bob commented to Herman. "I've got their number right now. Think they're goin' to come and make fun of us country people. The first move any of 'em makes I'll crash this fiddle over his head."

Bob was amazed to see the young man and his friends speaking cordially to everyone present and joining in the square dances. When Bob played and sang "St. Louis Blues," the young man joined him in the chorus with a voice that was surprisingly good. Later in the evening he introduced himself. He was Milton Brown, a young cigar salesman.

Bob and Milton became close friends. Whenever Bob played for a dance Milton came. It was a friendship that was to last until Milton's death, but which was to bring many complications into Bob's life.

A Taste Of Fame Turns Sour

For seven weeks during the summer, KFJZ staged a fiddling contest. Thirteen bands competed and not one of them had less than five members with the exception of the Wills Fiddle Band, which was composed exclusively of Bob and Herman. The prize was a $50 gold piece.

It was not surprising that the Wills Fiddle Band won, for the simplicity of effect of just the fiddle and guitar working in perfect harmony was much more pleasing than the twanging of from five to nine men.

The presentation was to be made in a park. A great deal of publicity had been given the event which was to be broadcast and a record crowd was expected. Neither Bob nor Herman had any decent clothes to wear, so Bob announced that they would spend their money in advance buying an outfit. Herman protested. He said he needed the money for other things and that it was silly to spend it for clothes—especially silly to spend it before they had it. But Bob was smart enough to realize that appearance is very important and that if they ever expected to get ahead they had to look the part.

He dragged Herman to a clothing store and having convinced the merchant that their checks would be good the next day when they would deposit the gold piece, they purchased white trousers, white shirts, white shoes, new ties and straw hats. When the bill was added, there was just $1.60 apiece left of the money they were to receive that night.

Herman was still grumbling, but Bob was confident that they would look well and would be well received at the presentation. He was right. They were given a great ovation by the 7,000 people gathered in the park. He regretted the publicity when during the celebration party later in the evening, he heard an announcement over KTAT that another band had been put in the place of the program which he and Herman played. He had been found out at last.

A few afternoons later, Bob was awakened by a dejected, worried Milton. He had lost his job as cigar salesman.

"That's the best thing that ever happened to you," Bob exclaimed. "Why, you can make more money singing than you ever could selling cigars. Come on out to the medicine show tonight and I'll give you $5 to sing two songs."

Milton did and Bob gave him the $5, although it was half his salary. Milton attached himself to Bob then, believing that he really could accomplish something with his singing. In this fashion, Bob more or less acquired Milton's brother, Durwood, who was a youngster learning to play the guitar.

An "Aladdin Lamp" program was opening that fall over WBAP and was in search of talent. As their product was aimed for the farmers, the sponsors wanted a type of program that would appeal particularly to that group. They had square dancing programs in mind. Bob auditioned his little group and was hired.

There were a few days before the program was to open, so Bob, who had not been home for two years, and the others piled into Milton's coupe and drove to Lakeview. They played a dance in an old friend's house and the crowd that came was so large that many had to stand outside and just listen to the music. The return of Jim Rob and his magic fiddle was an irresistible lure.

When the new program opened, the sponsors let Bob know that they did not want Milton to sing. Bob tried to use him as a square dance caller. Finally, he decided that the sponsors did not know what they wanted and began to play comical songs, old folk songs and run the program as he liked. Fan mail flooded the station.

Bob felt that they could make more money if they would play for dances several nights a week in one spot. He found Crystal Springs, which was rather run down, but at least the manager offered to hire them. His guarantee was $2 apiece every night they played. The boys were eager to accept this offer and argued against Bob's idea of going in on a percentage basis. Bob was beginning to see ahead. He knew that if they were as good as he thought they were, they could draw big crowds. The boys were grateful later for his insistence on the percentage, as the first night they made $11 apiece and on the second Saturday night $19.

Only Herman and Milton were with him on the radio program, but for the dance band he added Durwood and Sleepy Johnson, a banjo player that he had met and liked. During this period he unwittingly trained a member of his present band. Jesse Ashlock was a youngster who devotedly followed Bob everywhere. When there was an errand to be run, he was there to do it. Flattered by the boy's attention and hero worship, Bob gave him a $50 fiddle and showed him how to use it. The others thought Jesse a nuisance and groaned whenever he appeared at one of their dances proudly nursing his new fiddle. But Bob occasionally let him play a simple tune with them and encouraged him.

As the "Aladdin Laddies" and the Crystal Springs dance band, Bob's little group was doing fairly well. But Bob was ambitious for more radio programs. The Burrus Mills and Elevator Co. was a large concern and Bob had met several people connected with it in minor capacities. Through them he managed to persuade the company to pay for a radio line to a special dance one night in return for advertising its flour. During the broadcast he called the band "The Light Crust Doughboys," a name which he originated. He was using the song "Eagle Ridin' Papa" on his Aladdin program with special words, so he wrote another set using it as a theme song for the "Doughboys." Burrus Mills still uses that theme song, but the events of the next month did not forecast a long life for it.

The company was sufficiently impressed with the dance experiment to allow Bob to play an early morning program for it over KFJZ. However, it was not impressed enough to pay the boys a salary for it. Bob felt that it would eventually realize that the program was good advertising. This confidence was not justified when at the end of the month they were notified that the program would be discontinued because it was not a success.

The station continued the program regardless, still on a no pay basis. So much fan mail came in that Bob decided to confront W. Lee O'Daniel, general manager and president of the mills, in an attempt to persuade him to not only take them back but pay them for it this time. It did not occur to him to look for another sponsor. He had set out to get the flour company's sponsorship and he was determined to win, no matter what the odds. The one thing in his mind was that an affiliation with a big company meant a steady job. He considered the dances an uncertain source of income and fully expected them to die as quickly as they had flourished. He had no idea that they would continue at Crystal Springs for two years and that later, dances would become the most important factor in his professional life. What he wanted and thought best now, was to work with a company in some capacity or other while playing radio programs for it on the side.

Hubbin' It

Bob pushed his way into O'Daniel's inner office and waited patiently for recognition. O'Daniel, an impressive figure, continued to busy himself with papers on his desk. In a few minutes he said coldly, "What did you want to talk to me about?"

"The main thing is, I want a job," Bob blurted. "I'll drive a truck, sweep the floor or anything. But I want a job."

"So you want to work?" O'Daniel said amusedly. "It's out of the ordinary for a musician to want to work, isn't it?"

"I've always worked and I sure know what hard work is," Bob retorted indignantly.

"Well, that puts a different light on it if you're sure you want to work."

O'Daniel was silent a minute or two, and then offered to take on the program again paying each of the boys $7.50 a week. In addition to that, Bob would have to drive a flour truck every day, Herman would join the bull gang loading and doing heavy work, and Milton would call on bakers pushing sales.

If Bob had not already known what hard work was, he would have soon found out. Every morning at 7 he played the program. During the day he averaged 100 miles in his truck. Four nights a week he played at Crystal Springs for dances. These dances grew increasingly popular as it was noised about that the players were the Light Crust Doughboys. Bob was unaware that the radio job benefited the dances. It was his conviction that the more publicity they received the sooner people would tire of them.

Their salaries were raised to $15 during the second month and remained at that figure for a year. What O'Daniel did not give them in money he soon gave them in personal attention, following the day Bob persuaded him to say a few words during the program. With Bob's approval he took up writing the continuity. He went Doughboy crazy. He sought their friendship. He bought a white automobile with flamboyantly painted advertisements of the program covering it. He fitted it up with loud speakers and arranged for the boys to make good will tours playing in all the nearby towns. He sent them to chamber of commerce programs and special occasions everywhere. Many days Bob would pick up his fiddle at 7 A.M. and not have it out of his hand until 1 A.M. the next morning.

A Taste Of Fame Turns Sour

O'Daniel frequently presented poems he had written and requested the boys to compose tunes to them and use the results on the program. In this way such songs as "Beautiful Texas," "Your Own Sweet Darling Wife," "I Want Somebody To Cry Over Me," and "Put Me In Your Pocket" were introduced. O'Daniel was particularly addicted to timely songs. The fall of a flu epidemic he wrote a song of which the chorus went "Kachoo! Kachoo! Kachoo!" When Jimmie Rodgers, the famous cowboy singer, died, the O'Daniel-Doughboy combination created a song in his memory. There was a dirge lamenting the "Fall of '29." The morning that Roosevelt was inaugurated in 1932 O'Daniel arrived three hours before broadcast time with a poem, "On to Victory Mr. Roosevelt," which he wanted set to music and played that day. As he read the words, Bob played a tune on the fiddle which fitted perfectly. The engineer recorded it and then Bob had to spend an hour and a half learning his own composition from the record, for he could not remember it.

O'Daniel switched the program from KFJZ to a 12:30 spot on WBAP. Six months later he hooked up WOAI San Antonio and KPRC Houston. Then he added evening programs over the southwest quality network which included KTAT and KOMA Oklahoma City. Thus the Doughboys became known throughout several states.

Three days after this new hook-up a crisis arose—Milton resigned. It was the beginning of another black period for Bob when everything would seem to go wrong. The future was to look as uncertain and unpromising as it had looked assured and hopeful when O'Daniel became interested in them.

There had been a change in the Doughboy personnel almost a year before the Milton trouble occurred. Prestige and financial security had gone to Herman's head making him careless to the point where it was necessary for Bob to replace his guitar playing with that of Sleepy Johnson, who was playing with them at Crystal Springs. Milton's case was different. It was a clash between two strong personalities. Milton was a leader as was Bob. He wanted to run the program, but Bob's self-confidence that the success of the group depended upon his leadership was even stronger than that of Milton's. The two were still good friends, but their professional rivalry increased until Bob decided that it should be brought into the open. He went to O'Daniel and told him that one or the other of them would have to go. "I'm perfectly willing to leave," Bob said. "I can always get along, but you'll have to make your choice."

O'Daniel was unwilling to fire Milton with no obvious provocation, so he made him a proposition. He offered him $25 a week if he would not play for the Crystal Springs dances, reserving his performances exclusively for the mill. Bob had previously accepted the same offer. O'Daniel felt that it would not appeal to Milton as he had already asked for twice the amount of salary and wanted his brother to be given Sleepy's place.

Milton resigned and immediately started a program with his own band at KTAT. Bob had known he was organizing the band, but since he did not mention it, Bob said nothing also. Milton was prepared for the break, but Bob was not.

For a week after Milton's sudden departure Bob managed to keep the program going as best he could, but drove night and day between broadcasts trying to find a good singer. He listened to dozens but none suited him. A Tommy Duncan had called him for an audition. Thinking it was a singer he had heard and did not like, he refused. The second time that Tommy called, he was so discouraged in his search that he consented to listen to him. The moment Tommy began to sing Bob became excited. He was not sure, but perhaps his search was ended. He listened to him sing from 9:30 in the evening until 3 in the morning. Finally, he asked him if he could sing "I Ain't Got Nobody."

"That's my favorite song," Tommy said.

"If you can sing it the way I have in mind it should be sung, you've got a job," Bob replied.

Tommy sang it that way. He is with Bob today.

The addition of Tommy to the group did not completely satisfy Bob. He added Kermit Whalen, a bass fiddle player, and wanted another guitar. He still saw Herman every day, although no mention had been made about rehiring him. Herman was walking the streets and Bob kept him supplied with small change. Bob felt that perhaps he had learned a lesson. Perhaps the experience had made a man of him. They had a long talk. Herman was humble. He promised that if Bob would take him back, he would never do anything to displease him again. He had found out about himself now. He knew what he should do and should not.

When Bob told O'Daniel that he was taking Herman back, the general manager objected. "When I fire a man he stays fired," he commented.

"That's not my way of doing things," Bob retorted. "You didn't hire Herman and you didn't fire him. I did that. If I can make a man out of a fellow I take him back. I'm going to take Herman back whether you pay him or not. I'll pay him out of my own salary."

O'Daniel relented at the end of the first week Herman played and gave him $5. Bob added a little so that he could live. Herman continued and nothing more was said. After a few months O'Daniel paid him $12.50 a week.

A year went by without many difficulties but the boys were complaining to Bob about their salaries. They were required to stay at the mill eight hours a day rehearsing. They were not allowed to make any additional money by playing dances or outside engagements. They were expected to live well and present an appearance compatible with the fame of the Doughboys. It was an impossibility. Bob, as the leader, was only making $28, Sleepy $25, Tommy $17.50, Kermit $15 and Herman the $12.50. Whenever he could, Bob gave them money from his larger salary, but he had to support not only his wife and little girl, but send as much money as possible to his family on the farm.

Up to this time O'Daniel and Bob got along well together. A rift appeared between them when Bob pressed him for higher salaries for the boys. Although they liked each other personally and each admired the other, they could not find a common meeting ground as far as business was concerned. The beginning of the end was a quarrel they had over Bob's brother, Johnnie Lee.

O'Daniel had put Johnnie Lee, eight years Bob's junior, to work driving a mill truck for $12 a week. Part of this salary, like Bob's, went back to the Wills family. Johnnie Lee owed a $4 bill at a grocery store run by a crochety old woman. When she was unable to collect the bill, she complained to the mill superintendent. The old man stormed at Johnnie Lee and threatened to fire him. As a large number of truck drivers had already been laid off, due to the stores being overstocked with flour, Johnnie Lee went to Bob for advice. Bob took the matter to O'Daniel.

"I can't do anything about it, Bob," O'Daniel said. "It's the president of this country that's responsible for this business condition. Look at all these poor truck drivers. I know they only make small salaries, but it's all we can afford to pay. Why, we're going to have to shut the mills down for a few weeks and lay everybody off because of business conditions. I wish there were something I could do about it, but there isn't. I don't know what's the matter with the world."

"I can tell you," Bob said firmly. "In the first place we'll take Johnnie Lee's case. That old lady is too old to run a grocery store. She don't know how to handle business right. Her son or some young fellow in her family should be runnin' it for her. And that old man you have for a superintendent. He should be retired and a young fellow put in his place, too. If some of the people wouldn't take all the big salaries and give us workin' people better wages, we wouldn't have to fight to pay our bills. We could live decent. It ain't the president that's all wrong. It's the people gettin' the big salaries and not doin' nothin' but shake their heads over the workin' folks who are starvin' to death. If it weren't for them kind of old men this old world wouldn't be in no condition like it is!"

Bob demanded that he and Johnnie Lee be fired immediately. "We can do as well as the truck drivers you've already laid off," he said hotly.

"Bob, you're out of your head," O'Daniel said calmly. "You come back tomorrow and talk to me when you've cooled down."

When Bob returned the next day O'Daniel announced he had raised his salary to $38 a week and that Johnnie Lee would not be fired.

Two days later O'Daniel called Bob into his office and announced that he wanted him to organize the best band in the country. "If it takes 17 men to do it right hire them," he declared. "I want to put this program over like it's never been put over before!"

Bob privately resolved to stay in line in the hope that things could be worked out under this new declaration of O'Daniel's faith in him. As none of the boys, including himself, could read music, he decided to find someone who could, to play the new tunes so that they could memorize them. He had met a candy salesman who was a good pianist with a musical education. Although he did not want to use him in the band, he thought it an excellent move to hire him. He figured that when not rehearsing, he could take Johnnie Lee's place driving a truck, thus leaving Johnnie Lee, who played the guitar fairly well, free to become a Doughboy. He believed that this would appeal to the general manager because it would be increasing the payroll by only one man but doubling the value of the band.

When he presented the idea O'Daniel turned it down. "I'll never permit your brother to be in the band," he said. "Brothers don't work well together. They're never successful."

Bob argued, but O'Daniel was firm.

That night the legalization of beer in Texas went into effect and the whole town was celebrating. Bob and the boys took their instruments and wandered from beer tavern to beer tavern helping the rest of Ft. Worth drink up all the beer and playing wherever they went. O'Daniel, who had come to the conclusion that he and Bob could not work together any more, fired Bob for his part in the celebration and failure to appear for the following day's program.

Nothing was said about Bob's dismissal to the boys as O'Daniel had asked him to stay for a few days until he had put on a special program launching a "Save Your Own Life Club" which the group had been rehearsing for a week. O'Daniel made arrangements for Clifford Gross, a Kentucky fiddler, to take Bob's place. This gave Bob bitter amusement as Gross had taken his place once before—the time KTAT had discovered he was working for another radio station as well as its own.

After the special program, Bob walked out without a word to O'Daniel or the boys. He was discouraged. He was back where he had been three years before when he and Herman had started out so bravely. He would have to begin all over again.

As he walked away from the mill wondering what his next move should be, he remembered that all his clothes and possessions were in the studio and turned back. O'Daniel was talking to the boys, but as Bob walked in there was complete silence.

"Well, don't let me interrupt you," Bob said. "I just come back to get my clothes."

"I was telling the boys that we'll have to carry on just as though you were still with us," O'Daniel explained.

"Why, of course. Why shouldn't you? I'm not going to bother you. You're a million dollar corporation. You don't have to make any explanations to a man who ain't got nothin'."

O'Daniel wished him success "although it will be tough sledding" and left.

Silently Bob gathered his things. Then Tommy spoke, "Where do we go from here?"

"What do you mean ?".

"I mean that I'm goin' with you. The reason you was fired was that you made trouble sticking up for us tryin' to get more money. You hired me. O'Daniel didn't. And I'm not leavin' you until you do fire me. Anywhere you go I'm goin'."

"That goes for me," Kermit chimed in.

"You boys are gettin' a little hasty," Bob said slowly. "Let's don't go anywhere. You've got a job here. You're gettin' money that gives you a chance to eat and maybe feed me a hamburger once in awhile. Let's just leave things like they are."

His argument did not convince them. They were firm in their decision.

Herman and Sleepy said that they would like to go with him but that, after all, as he had pointed out, they had responsibilities and did not feel it would be to their advantage to give up their positions. However, if he managed to find something to do, they would be glad to come with him then.

Bob paid little attention to them. He was concerned with Tommy and Kermit. It was unbelievable that they were so loyal. He argued with them until he was convinced that they really meant it. Then he instructed all the boys to mention not a word of the discussion, but to play the program that night and he would get in touch with them the next day.

It was Saturday. Bob had to think fast. He had no money and no prospects. The loyalty of the two boys banished his discouragement, but it had been replaced by desperation. He had to do something! They had not

72

let him down. He could not let them down. Then he thought of Waco. There might be a chance there.

That afternoon he was in conference with Everett Stover, manager of station WACO. He talked him into giving them a 12:30 spot, which was in direct competition with the Doughboy program. Of course Bob would not be paid, but that made no difference.

He was confident that just being on the air would enable him to find a sponsor and to receive enough publicity to make dances profitable. He looked up a fireman friend, Bill Little, and explained his predicament. Little not only loaned him $25 to bring the boys to Waco, but said he would book dances for them around town.

It was late Sunday night when Bob returned to Ft. Worth, sleepless, unshaven, but triumphant. He routed Tommy, Kermit, and Johnnie Lee out of bed. He told them what he had done and demanded to know again whether they would stick with him no matter what happened now. He had told the station that he would let it know definitely whether he would return or not Monday morning. He wanted to be sure of the boys first. The boys reassured him vehemently. Kermit said his brother, June, who played guitar, would come with them, too.

Bob instructed them to resign Monday morning, but to play the daily program. He told Johnnie Lee to resign at the same time, continuing to drive the truck until noon while the mill found someone to replace him. O'Daniel would find himself without a program, for only Herman and Sleepy would be left. Their function had been to play accompaniment. The others had provided the personality and singing—the things that made the program popular.

O'Daniel was angry when he was informed what was to happen. He offered Tommy and Kermit salary raises if they would remain, but their loyalty was not to be shaken. O'Daniel then sent Johnnie Lee to get the Doughboy car and deliver it to him. Bob had made $80 payment on the car on the understanding that it was to be his. When he heard that O'Daniel had sent for it, his anger came to a head. He stormed into the mill office demanding to know whether the car was his or not. An official suggested he see O'Daniel.

"I'll see him," Bob roared. "But tell him he'll have to come out here. I'm not goin' to go to him."

HUBBIN' IT

O'Daniel appeared, asking him to come into his office.

"All right, seeing as how you've come out here first and asked me in, I'll come," Bob yelled.

O'Daniel offered to settle the car dispute for $100 and Bob accepted. As he wrote out the check, he said, "You're making the worst mistake in your life, Bob. You are taking these boys from a job where they make money. You're taking them with you where they probably won't make a dime. This will go down in history against you, Bob."

"O'Daniel, it may go down in history, but it won't go down against me! I'm not takin' these boys. No, sir! If I was, I would have somethin' to be ashamed of. But you listen to me. These boys are comin' to me because they want to. I didn't ask them. They're leavin' a million dollar concern to go with a guy like me who you say ain't got nothin'. But I must have somethin' or they wouldn't come. I'm proud of myself. I've got somethin' to be proud of and those boys will get a break because I'll kill myself workin' to see that they do!"

It was thus that Bob and O'Daniel parted in September 1933. It was not to be their last meeting.

Chapter Eight

Before The Dawn

The gentle dew that drops from heaven aroused feelings in them that were far from gentle the first dance that they played in Waco. It dampened the courage with which they opened their new campaign to fight back. They played in an open air place on the outskirts of town and the heavy dew broke $36 worth of instrument strings. Five dollars was all they cleared at the gate, as the large crowd preferred to sit in automobiles listening to the music rather than to pay to dance.

Bad luck seemed ready to set up housekeeping with them, for the second dance they played, the police closed at 10 P.M. Bill, the fireman booker, had arranged it within the city limits without procuring a permit. Bill broken-heartedly offered to go to jail if the police would allow them to finish. The dance was closed in spite of such generosity. So Bob announced that he would play a free dance the following night when they obtained a permit. A tremendous crowd showed up and the boys played sadly seeing so many people with no money coming in.

Within a few weeks things changed. They made friends and their dances were increasingly popular. They played for clubs and civic organizations. They were booked for performances in the largest theater in Waco.

One day Bob was served with papers informing him that a suit had been filed against him by Burrus Mills for $10,000. The mill claimed damages because Bob and the boys stated in advertising their dances and performances that they were formerly the Light Crust Doughboys. The petition claimed that this constituted unfair competition and an infringement of the mill's rights to the trademark name; that it led the public to believe that the mill was sponsoring or approving public dances and had injured it in various other ways.

75

HUBBIN' IT

Bob hired Stafford and Goodall, two young lawyers just out of college, to defend him. The great amount of newspaper publicity about the suit helped his business, but made him no happier over the matter.

The trial was held in district court in Waco. O'Daniel was present with a battery of lawyers from Ft. Worth and Dallas. Their eloquence was of little use, for Burrus Mills lost the case. It was appealed to the civil court of appeals. An opinion was not given until June, 1935, but the district court's decision was upheld.

At Christmas time Bob decided that all the flowers had been picked in that particular field. They had played four months and done well, not only because of the unwanted publicity but because it had been a good cotton season. Cotton was the chief source of income in Waco territory and Bob realized that after Christmas money would be scarce. He knew from hard experience how the seasons went. If they continued, it was an inevitability that they would be forced to disband. He made his plans to come to Oklahoma. When the Doughboy program had been broadcast from KOMA Oklahoma City quantities of fan mail had been received from that area. The majority of it was addressed to Bob personally. He figured that there would be enough interest in his personality there to keep them from starving to death.

He had expanded his organization by four men during the four months. The fireman's brother-in-law, O.W. Mayo, had shown an interest in Bob and made a good booking for him. He had accompanied them to the dance and worked on the door selling tickets. Gradually, he worked more and more with Bob until they came to an agreement that he would work exclusively with him as a booking and business manager. He is with him today. Bob had also added his cousin, Son Lansford, who played both guitar and fiddle, and another guitar player. Then there was Everett Stover, the manager of WACO, who had given Bob his first break in the strange territory. About the time Bob was planning to leave for Oklahoma Everett lost his job, so Bob asked him to join their group as an announcer. He did not know that Everett was a good performer on the trumpet and that he used to direct the governor's band in Austin and at one time played in the New Orleans symphony orchestra. When he did discover it, Everett became a part of the band and is now his right hand man in announcing programs and directing rehearsals or performances when Bob is not present.

Mayo argued with Bob against going to Oklahoma, pointing out that they were doing well in Waco making as much as $170 a night and it would be foolish to go where they could not be sure of the possibilities of succeeding.

"Mayo, of course I want you to go with me," Bob said. "But if you or any of the other boys don't want to go you can stay. I'm leavin'. I'm goin' places and nothin' can stop me. This is a little old hundred watt radio station here and folks outside of 20 miles away can't hear us. The cotton money is all gone. It's goin' to be tough country to live in until next fall. I'm goin' someplace where everybody can know me and I'm goin' to the top. If you fellows want to gamble with me you can come, but if you don't I want you to make up your minds and stay here and stay now—not be comin' back full of hard feelings because I didn't tell you what things might be like."

There was no further discussion. Nobody wanted to stay behind. Bob made a quick trip to Oklahoma City alone to see if he could make the arrangements he had in mind with WKY. He left the program director under no misapprehension as to what his connection with the mill had been and the resultant lawsuit. The station agreed to give him some time and he went back for the boys. There was no money in the deal, but Bob hoped to find a sponsor once they were heard on the air.

Their farewell radio program in Waco brought such a crowd to the building to tell them good-bye that it was two hours before they could leave after the program. They piled light-heartedly into a recently acquired old seven-passenger sedan, which had formerly belonged to a governor of Texas, but which they had found required more man power than gasoline to push it.

Once in Oklahoma City, Bob spent all their money advertising their arrival and booking dances. For the first time they used the name "Bob Wills and His Texas Playboys." Bob had called the group "Playboys" in Waco. It was a natural adaptation since they had been called "Doughboys" for so long and thought of themselves always as the "boys."

They had played only five programs when the station announced that they would no longer be allowed to play. It was dickering with the mill for a contract.

HUBBIN' IT

Knowing the difficulties Bob and the mill had experienced, it felt that a politic move would be to discontinue relationship with the "Playboys."

That was the most downcast period of Bob's life. He was far from home and the support of his Texas friends. He had only enough money to tide the group over a few days. He had the responsibility of each boy on his conscience. It was not now a question of making good money for them. It was a question of feeding them. Despairingly he cancelled all the dance engagements that had been made, believing that without radio publicity they would be unable to draw a crowd. They were an unknown group of musicians whose only assets at the moment were unnoticed talents and exceedingly healthy appetites.

Discouraged and desperate they drove into Tulsa. Bob went to William B. Way, manager of KVOO, and explained their situation in detail. He asked him, as he had asked the other stations, for radio time—no salaries. Way said he felt there was a chance for a band like Bob's to make good in that territory and agreed to help. Bob played his first program over KVOO that same midnight.

The band was at least being heard again, but conditions were stringent. Bob rented one room in an apartment basement and the nine of them slept there, some in the beds and some on the floor. They ate the usual beans that are an invariable part of hard times. These conditions lasted a month before the sunlight of better finances broke the gloom.

For two weeks they played an alternate morning and evening spot on the air and spent the rest of the time rehearsing. It was an uneasy, anxious period. Not only was no money coming in, but Way was negotiating with the mill for a program. Bob was fearful that once again the mill's competition would be too strong for him. He soon discovered that Way was not interested in taking him off the air. The fan mail that was coming in predicted that he was going to be a hit. Once again O'Daniel and Bob clashed on the business battleground. Both their programs were carried by KVOO. They were destined to meet and disagree only once more.

Bob could have obtained engagements playing in "joints" of unsavoury reputation, but in spite of the fact that they could find no other jobs, he refused. He knew in his heart the high level to which he wanted to build the band. He knew that if he cheapened it in the beginning, the fight up would be almost impossible. He did not have to hold out long, for at the end of two tough weeks he had arrangements for a big dance in Oilton. That dance was a success. From then on it was easier. They played engagements in other small towns and soon were playing all over the state.

In September 1934 KVOO signed a year's contract with Crazywater Crystals for a program from 12:30 to 1 P.M. on the condition that Bob would play it. Bob was to receive no pay, but he accepted the program as he felt that to play that particular time over the air would do more than anything else toward building up his reputation. That half hour will catch listeners of every type. Business men and laborers are eating in restaurants and lunch stands where radios are blaring. Housewives have finished their morning work. School children are home for lunch. The farmer and his wife have left the chores for the noon day meal and invariably listen to the radio. The young men and women who do nothing but play, forming a goodly percentage of a dance crowd, are awake after a long night's pleasure. There are few people whom such a time does not reach.

During the fourteen months that Bob played this program, he was building his organization. The average band leader does not feel that he can change his organization for the better unless he is able to finance it. Bob could not think that way. He was making money, yes, but not enough money to hire the best musicians. Yet he refused to keep the band the same. He knew that if he did not grow and change for the better, he would lose his popularity. The novelty of his music would wear off and the public fancy, always so fickle, would be caught by someone else.

The boys that he had with him were good fellows but their capabilities were not yet developed enough. Tommy was only adequate on the piano, a job which he had taken over in addition to his singing. Son, who was playing bass fiddle, had never seen one until he came to Oklahoma. Johnnie Lee could strum only a few chords on the banjo. So Bob worked harder than ever before to cover up with his clowning, his fiddle, his chatter and his personality, the inability of the band as far as real musicianship was concerned. Other musicians criticized him, called him "dumb" and predicted that he would not last. They did not realize that he was using superb showmanship to sell mediocre performances. And he sold them! The boys were not loafing behind his front. They were studying, practicing and developing.

The change from a fiddle band to one including brass sections, drums and piano was not intentional. These additions were made as casually as the original change occurred. Everett had been under the illusion that he was hired not only as an announcer, but as a trumpet player. He surprised Bob, who knew nothing of his musical ability, by appearing with his trumpet and joining in the tunes. As the lone trumpet blended nicely and sounded well, Bob said nothing. He no longer had a fiddle band.

A few months after they arrived and their improved finances enabled them to move into a roomier apartment, Bob noticed that they were being joined in rehearsals by the son of the apartment house manager. This plump, spectacled, quiet youngster, Zeb McNally, played the saxophone. He played so well that Bob did not object to his rehearsing with them, although he usually angrily dismisses rehearsals if a stranger persists in horning in.

One night when one of the boys was unable to play, Zeb asked if he might take his place. Bob agreed and paid him $5. Then Zeb played radio programs with them. During the summer time when the boys took brief vacations, Zeb filled in—always on the $5 a night basis. Finally, Zeb was going along to dances with them whether or not any of the boys were absent. He was playing every radio program and every dance. At this point Bob remonstrated with him, saying that he could not afford to have him go all the time and that they did not need him. Zeb asked if he might go one more night. Bob consented. However, the next day Zeb was present at the radio broadcast. After the program as the boys were putting their instruments in the bus to be ready for the night jaunt, Bob called Zeb aside.

"You'd better go get your instrument out of the car, Zeb," he said. "You can't go with us any more. I told you that before, but I guess you don't understand me."

"Bob, you don't need to pay me $5 a night," Zeb said pleadingly. "Just give me a dollar a night and let me go with you. That's more than I'd make playing around here anyway."

"Why, you couldn't live decent on $6 a week. I wouldn't pay a man that little."

"Oh, I can get along fine on that much. Really I can. Please Bob, just let me go with you and only pay me a dollar."

Zeb pleaded so eloquently that Bob agreed to let him go another night, but paid him the usual $5. Zeb continued to go everywhere with the band in spite of what Bob would tell him. He worked so hard and his arrangements were so pleasing that finally Bob said no more to him. He could not fire him as he had never hired him. Zeb has never officially been hired, yet he is with Bob today. Bob has raised his pay time and again, but nothing has ever been said about his position with the band since.

The permanent acquisition of Zeb made Bob realize that he would have to hire a drummer to balance the two horns so the music would sound fuller. One night he noticed a young fellow at the dance listening and watching intently. He could tell that he was a musician, but what kind he did not know. After the dance the young fellow introduced himself. He was a drummer by the name of Smokey Dacus. Smokey had played with several bands but could not find a position that satisfied him. He had heard of Bob Wills and thought he would ask him for a job. Bob was dubious as to whether he would fit in the organization as he was a modern style musician, but Smokey was so eager to be given a chance to adapt himself that Bob hired him. He is still hitting licks for Bob.

Herman came back into the fold. Bob was visiting in Ft. Worth when he heard on a Friday that Herman was to be fired from the Doughboy group the next day. He immediately went to Herman and told him to hand in his resignation and come to work for him. Herman did so and did not know until two years later that Bob had saved him the humiliation of being fired. Not long afterwards Sleepy quit the Doughboys and Bob hired him. The old triumvirate was now reunited and still is.

There were to be more reunions of the old Ft. Worth days. He hired Jesse, the youngster whom he taught how to play. Then he acquired Al Stricklin, a Ft. Worth friend who had worked his way through Baylor university teaching piano. Then there was Leon McAuliffe, a guitarist. Leon had become a Doughboy after Bob's severance with the group. Herman recommended him to Bob. It has always been Bob's policy never to hire a man away from another band, although other band leaders have never been that thoughtful of him. They have often tried to hire his boys but never succeeded. Although he needed a guitarist he would not offer the position to Leon while he was still a Doughboy. However, Jesse was making a trip to Ft. Worth and Bob told him to see Leon and comment that if at any time he needed a job there was a possibility Bob might consider him. The day that Jesse looked him up, Leon was playing his last program as a Doughboy. He had handed in his resignation two weeks earlier. So he immediately came to Bob and is now one of the most popular members of the band.

The band had grown to 12 members. They had a bus of their own. There was more extra money in their pockets than they had ever had the pleasure of jingling before. Fan letters were increasing. Dances were crowded. But the Crazywater Crystal contract was drawing to a close. Something else must be figured out to keep their names before the radio audience.

It was then that O'Daniel appeared in his final role. He was no longer with the Ft. Worth flour mill. Extremely conscious of Bob's popularity and drawing power, he came to him with a proposition. He wanted to go into partnership with Bob and sponsor flour. The idea was not a new one to Bob. He had been thinking of the same thing, but had not gone into details. O'Daniel discovered that Bob would not consider taking him into partnership or working with him in any way. They had differed too much in the past for Bob to feel that they could work together in the future. In a friendly fashion they parted for the last time.

Bob's approach to the flour deal he had been thinking of was unique in the history of radio and advertising. Before he contacted the Red Star Milling Co., which he had selected as the company he wanted to work with, he had a conference with KVOO manager Way. He told him that if he could arrange the deal with the flour company, he would like to buy his own radio time. He wanted the 12:30 spot that he had been playing for a year. He would pay for the time himself and advertise a new brand of flour from which he would get a percentage of every barrel sold. He would be the only advertising medium for it. Instead of the usual procedure of a company buying radio time and hiring talent to sell its product, Bob was offering talent and time in exchange for a product. For the first time a radio program could prove with exact figures how many people it influenced, as it would be brand new to the market. Sales would increase solely because of Bob's selling power.

Way was so impressed with this unusual idea that he assured Bob he would hold the time open for him while he found out what the Red Star people thought about it. It only took the flour people a week to sign a contract on Bob's terms. They had never heard of such an arrangement, but it was to their advantage. Here was a chance to sell more flour with no advertising expense, other than a small percentage of each barrel's value. If it flopped, they would not suffer.

It was a serious venture for Bob. His radio time would cost him around $12,000 a year. He had wilfully cut his chances of selling large quantities of flour by insisting that the flour be of first rate quality. He could have made a better deal and sold a cheaper flour by taking a second grade brand. He did not want his name to be associated with anything that was not the best. He felt that it would mean more business to him over a period of years although it would cut profits. It was not a certainty that he could make even enough money to pay for the radio time. He was gambling on the expressions of good will that thousands of dance customers and radio fans had made to him. He was gambling on his ability to sell the public as he thought they would like to be sold—simply, good-humoredly without flowery language and high pressure salesmanship.

Play Boy flour went on the market in November 1935. Play Boy bread was soon added. Within a few months sales shot to the top of the graph. Within two years flour sales have equaled company brands that have been on the market for 40 years.

Bob's gamble brought him into his own.

CHAPTER NINE

"PATHS OF GLORY"

Ten years have passed since the day Bob stood in the field pulling cotton bolls and deciding that he would work towards a band of his own. He has passed his goal further than he dreamed possible. Today, he is the most important figure in the entertainment world in the southwest. His fan mail averages a thousand letters a week. The phonograph records he has made for Brunswick Record Corporation head the list of national best sellers in its thirty-five cent class. People drive hundreds of miles to attend his dances. He receives the personal adulation of a hero.

Yet the old spirit of dissatisfaction is stronger than ever. He is working harder than he did when he picked seven hundred pounds of cotton a day. His discontent does not lie in greed for additional fame and money, but in the desire to give more to the people. He is continually working to improve, to study the public and change with it.

His primary problem is the personnel of his band. Without the proper building materials, the architect's plan cannot be carried out. Bob cannot give the public the things he wants to, unless he has the right sort of men working behind him on the band stand.

His policy has always been to hire a man, not just because he is a musician, but because of his personality and character. There are a great many excellent musicians to be had, but they are likely to be either of low morale or so "professional" that they would refuse to be molded into the unusual type of organization that is Bob's. A musician working for Bob Wills has to play everything from the latest swing tunes to religious music and old-time fiddling numbers. He has to entertain audiences that are a conglomeration drawn from every strata of American life. He has to be master of the secret of being truly democratic. He has to work harder than the average musician. It is no wonder that Bob considers true character a more important asset than unusual talent.

Once Bob has hired a man, he gives him the opportunity to make his position with the band what he will just so long as he stays "in harness" and works for the organization rather than for himself. For example, two years ago, he added Joe Ferguson, an Oklahoma lad, to the band as a singer. He was particularly impressed with Joe's attitude and personality. Joe sang well, but he became interested in the bass fiddle and learned how to play it. Now Joe would rather play the bass fiddle than sing, although he does both.

Bob has refused to build his band on a cold-blooded basis, but has assumed the role of a father raising a large family. If any of the boys get out of line, Bob gives him a private, verbal spanking. When that is finished, he will not allow pouting. One pouting musician will spoil the harmony of the entire band and it can no longer entertain an audience. If the musician continues to be temperamental, Bob will use severer methods even if he has to discharge him. He will perhaps give him another chance, if the man can show he is worthy of it. There are several members of the present band whom he has rehired, overlooking a past disagreement, and those boys are the ones who most openly praise him and show their intense loyalty.

The one thing he will not tolerate is professional jealousy. That will disorganize and ruin a band more quickly than anything else. If he sees it cropping up he immediately thrashes it out with the boys involved. To prevent it, he does not feature one man more than another. His personal attentions are lavished on all alike. On trips to out-of-town dances there is no set arrangement as to which cars the boys ride in. They never know until the last minute with whom they are going. Consequently, there are no cliques in the band. One of the best proofs of Bob's care in this matter is that his brother, Johnnie Lee, is just "one of the boys." Johnnie Lee receives no more consideration than anyone else and the boys like him for it. Bob is proud of the way Johnnie Lee has kept his head and lived up to his share of the agreement so well.

Soon Johnnie Lee will strike out on his own with a band under Bob's sponsorship. It is Bob's theory that an employer has a moral responsibility to the men he has hired and must look out for them more carefully during hard times even than during good ones. There are several members of his present band with whom he could dispense without hurting the popularity or musical appeal of the organization. Such a move would enable him to operate at less expense and maintain a surer economic status. But Bob would never let them go unless he knew they had good positions. Also, there are several of his relatives—a younger brother, Luther, and two cousins—who are good musicians and who are out of work. The strong family bond which is part of his heritage makes Bob feel as responsible for their welfare as for the boys whom he already employs. In order to take care of both groups he has decided to let them form a band under his banner with Johnnie Lee as leader. He will finance them and see that they get a good start in a new territory. It is not certain that they will succeed, but Bob feels strongly that if more employers would take a constructive and helpful attitude like this, there would be less chance of increasing unemployment.

Bob is a genuine father to his boys. They come to him for help in solving their problems. If they want a new car or a new home he arranges to finance it for them. If they have a headache or sore throat, he will not permit them to perform, but sends them immediately home to bed. If they have a fuss with their wives, Bob straightens things out. They depend upon him for everything.

Bob has his own philosophic reasons for such a state of affairs—reasons learned from working with cattle on the ranges and with mules on his farm. "If you have a bunch of sluggish cattle turned out on a run down pasture full of sand hills, you can't round 'em up," he says. "In the first place you ain't got nothin' worth roundin' up. But if you have a bunch of good high bred cattle feedin' in a pasture with a lot of good green grass and plenty of water, you can round 'em up quick. They'll go together and have a lot of life to 'em that makes it easier for you to handle a whole bunch. Then, too, if you've got some mules that ain't fed enough or well taken care of and treated right, and you try to make 'em plough cotton, why, they'll get about five or six acres a day done. But you take those same mules and feed 'em and treat 'em fine and then switch a harness on 'em and put 'em to a plow and they'll step out and plow 10 or 12 acres a day. Musicians are just the same way as them cattle and mules."

Bob treats his boys well, but he demands they "plow 10 or 12 acres a day." When they are "in harness" they must play to the best of their ability. They have a stern routine. Every day they play their broadcast from 12:30 P.M. to 1:15 P.M. Then in the late afternoon they start on a 50 to a 150 mile trip to play for a dance in Arkansas, Kansas, Missouri, Texas or Oklahoma. During the dance they never take an intermission. Bob figures that the people have paid their money for music and that they should get it every minute they are there. When one of the boys tires, he asks to be excused and wanders off for a smoke or a soft drink. They alternate absences, so that part of the band is playing all the time. Only the piano player, drummer and guitarists sit down to play. The others, like Bob, play on their feet. They feel the rhythm more strongly that way and can step up quickly for solos. Also, they do not become as tired as they would sitting down. They arrive home anywhere from 3 A.M. to 6 A.M. and are on the job again at noon. Several afternoons a week their free time is spent rehearsing new numbers. In addition to this regular routine there are many special engagements to be fulfilled at banquets, funerals and celebrations. Six days a week, every week in the year, that is their life.

For every 10 or 12 acres the boys plough a day, Bob ploughs a good 20 or 24. Not only is his routine the same as theirs, but he has a thousand responsibilities that they do not. Aside from looking out for them and solving the problems they present, he makes the decisions about the business, in connection with the flour, the dances and the radio. Mayo, his business manager, carries a great deal of this burden, but Bob keeps his finger on everything. There is nothing about the business that he does not know and no major decisions that he does not make. Almost all the profit that is made is reinvested in the band. He has bought his own dance hall in Tulsa, where he plays two nights a week and broadcasts daily. He has bought a sound truck which travels around the country playing his records and programs and advertising Play Boy bread and flour. He has bought two, big, white buses, fully equipped with the latest gadgets, to transport the boys from place to place. He does a great deal of charity work, playing benefit dances for worthy organizations.

The biggest problem of all is the one he is most grateful for—his public. The chief reason why Bob is so popular is that he is a superb showman who has not gone "big town" on the people. He is still a country boy. Bob is of the people, by the people and for the people. Consequently they adore him. They send him presents by the car load. His house is crammed with pillows, rugs, pennants, personal apparel, and knick knacks that they have made for him. Candy and cakes from some admiring housewife are always on hand. They paint pictures of him and write poems to him.

His vast fan mail is full of praise. He has received letters from strange places. A fellow living within 200 miles of the Arctic circle wrote him. The letter was a month on its way, part of the time by sled. Four men on Tincan Canoe island, near Australia, wrote a letter to him requesting him to play "Strawberry Roan," put it in a tin can and tossed it from a cliff into the Pacific Ocean where natives in canoes picked it up and carried it to a passing ship. It was the only method of mailing a letter they commanded.

His mail and his personal contacts bring him daily requests for help. All celebrities are approached in this way, but Bob's cases are different. The people have a naive faith that he will do what they ask, for they feel he really understands them and wants to help. He does and never fails them unless he discovers that they are trying to racketeer. That he will not stand. A girl stranded hundreds of miles from home will call on him for bus fare to return to her family. A grandmother wants money to get her grandchild because its parents are mistreating it. A young man wants a job because he has got his girl into trouble and they want to be married but have no money. A fellow is hungry and wants a place to sleep for the night. The troubles, disappointments, heartaches of thousands are poured into his ears. Because he has known so much trouble himself, he cannot refuse. His generosity is unlimited. A great deal of his money goes to his family. He has bought his father and mother a fine, big farm where they are extremely happy. He helps his brothers and sisters accomplish the things they desire. Hundreds of his relatives call on him—to tide them over until the next crop, to set them up in business, to do just about everything.

There are always demands on his personal time. An old man in Bixby, Oklahoma, who at one time was a fiddler, was dying. He told his daughter that he would like to hear the old tunes before he died and that he wished Bob Wills would play them for him. His daughter asked if she could hire Bob to give him a short concert, but Bob refused. Instead, he went to the old man's bedside and played tune after tune for more than an hour. It brought the color to the old fellow's cheeks and the life to his feet. When Bob left, he was sitting up in bed and in better health than he had been in months.

A woman was to celebrate her 110th birthday at a county poor farm. When Bob heard that her one request for a birthday present was for him to play for her, he took the entire band to the poor farm and put on a party for her.

These are only two of hundreds of such incidents. Bob is as generous with his time as his money. He wants to do these things because he is so grateful to the people. They have made it possible for him to accomplish what he has.

Another man could imitate his methods but could not duplicate his success because Bob is the possessor of an intangible quality—showmanship. He knows what the people want and he knows how to handle them. The reason why a dance crowd has a good time when he plays for it, is not because they are in a mood for a good time and anything could please them. It is because Bob molds their emotions and draws forth the proper reactions.

When Bob stands on the band stand and looks out over the crowd, his mind is not wandering. He is closely observing the people. In a few minutes he can. grade them like he used to grade bales of cotton. He looks at them and instantly figures out the kind of person they are and the type of music they would like to hear. When he calls to the band to play a number, it is not because it just happens to pop into his head. It is because that particular number will do to the crowd what he wants it to. He and the band have a repertoire of over 3,600 tunes, whereas the average band cannot play more than 50 upon a moment's notice. Thus, he has an infinite variety of material to suit any crowd.

If the crowd is composed mainly of youngsters who want to "swing it," Bob feeds it to them in ever increasing doses until he has them worked up to the point where anything he does is all right. Then he will play a slow, sweet interlude for the few in the audience that he knows are wondering if he can do it. In a few minutes he has picked up the tempo again for the majority of the crowd. He can play with people like he can with the fiddle changing their mood, pitch, intensity and tone.

Few bands in the country appeal to so many different types of people. The old folks come for square dance, jig time, schottische rhythms. The youngsters come for his popular, hot renditions. A smaller, more sophisticated crowd is drawn by the way he can show his mastery of smoother melodies.

No situations rise that he cannot handle. For example, the band played an engagement in the Osage country. The brother of Matt Kimes, one of Oklahoma's famous bank robbers, brought a crowd of hoodlums to the dance. They started to show off, waving guns in the air and shooting occasionally. The dance was turning into a regular Texas affair, the kind that Bob had experienced too often. One of the ruffians yelled to Bob, "You're in Osage country now, brother. We're tough." Bob answered calmly, "Hmph, I was raised where we done this in Sunday school," and went right on playing. He was not as calm as he pretended, but he kept his boys busy. When a couple of fighters would climb on the band stand, he would toss them back on the floor saying, "Keep your fights down there. This is our place up here."

Only occasionally does he lose his temper in public. Those times are provoked by men or women who become "smart alecky," and make themselves conspicuous by making fun of the crowd. Bob does not hesitate to point out the door to them. Sometimes he is amused by the antics of the dancers, but he would not think of poking fun at them. He will not allow anyone else to do it. To him, that is the most contemptible trick in the world. He bitterly opposes snobbishness. That attitude and the way he carries it out is just another reason why he is so popular.

Bob gives so freely of himself to the public that there is not much of him left to have a private life. He thinks of nothing but his work. His only relaxations are an occasional moving picture show and a physical work out with an ex-wrestler, Briggs, who accompanies him everywhere as a bouncer and general handy man.

The days when a $2 pawn shop fiddle looked good to him are very distant. The fiddle which he plays so gaily now is an old Guadagnini violin which once sold for $7,000 and which he purchased for $1,600. But he handles it with the same careless abandon as if it were a cheap pawn shop product.

In spite of all the "hubbin' it" he has done, Bob feels that life has been good to him and he is grateful. But he is driving himself on to accomplish the last goal which he has set.

"Paths Of Glory"

No orchestra has ever been known to quit at the pinnacle of its success. The entertainment business is pitifully full of has-beens hopelessly trying to make a come-back. Bob does not want that to happen to him or any of his boys.

Sometime in the future when the day arrives when he knows that he has given all he can give he wants to say good-bye before the public has a chance to tire of him. While he is still "tops" he will give one last, glorious, farewell dance and disappear.

By that time, he plans to have bought a big ranch where the land is fertile and cheap. Scattered around the main ranch will be smaller ones for each of his boys. Without him they could not make a living elsewhere. They are too dependent upon him. He wants them always close at hand where he can take care of them and still give them orders. They will form a self-sufficient little colony with their wives and children and there will be no worries in their old age, for Bob will supervise everything, seeing that the ranch is a success just as he has made the music business a success for them.

In the evenings they will gather in the main ranch house to talk. They will bring their instruments and strike up a tune or two. They will be Bob's own Texas Playboys and when the music rises, Bob will give one of his inimitable yells of "AH-haaa" which come only when he is pleased and happy and which have brought smiles to so many thousands.

Finis

Following are the songs which Bob Wills has composed and which are the favorites of thousands of his admirers. "Spanish Two Step" and "Maiden's Prayer" are two little fiddle tunes without words. "Oklahoma" is his tribute to the state where he has made his greatest success.

Spanish Two Step

By Bob Wills

Maidens Prayer

©y Bob Wills

Oklahoma

By Bob Wills

I where The Mis-tle-toe Grows In The Tree Tops And The Birds Sing Their
II As we Tra-vel The Beau-ti-ful High-Ways We Meet Go-od Friends

Sweet Mel-o-dies Ok-La-ho-ma's The State Of The Soo-Ner And Her
Ho-re And There Tran-cling Ov-er The Beau-ti-ful Moun-tains Where There's

cho

Peo-ple Are Al-ways Care-free I De-clare We Love It We're
Beau-ty Be-yond All Com-pare

Crazy A-bout It Ok-la-ho-ma We Love you, you Know And We'll

Ne-ver For-Get Your Good peo-ple And we'll praise you Wher-ev-er We

1st — 2nd — 3rd

Go — As We Go — Ok-La-Go — Te-xas Go

III Oklahoma's the home of the Indians,
Blessed with wealth both in soil and in oil,
Hospitality is always abundant,
And to you we'll always be loyal.

IV Texas sines of her Beautiful Texas,
Other states they all sine about,
Just come to Good old Oklahoma,
You will love it, we're sure theres
no doubt.

INDEX

INDEX

Foley, Emmaline. *See* Wills, Emmaline Foley

Gang fights, 35-37
Gassoway (medicine show head), 54
Great Depression, impact of, 60
Gross, Clifford, 71
Guadagnini violin, 90

Haines (smelter boss), working for, 26
Hedrick, Lawrence: working for, 26
Hoboing, 15-16, 20-23
Hoodlums, associating with, 33-37
Horse racing, 38-39
Hubbin' It (Sheldon)
    influence of, v
    interest in, vi
    qualities of, viii-ix
    themes in, vi-vii

"I Ain't Got Nobody," 68
Insurance company, working for, 42
"I Want Somebody To Cry Over Me," 67

Jim (medicine show), playing with, 55, 56, 57
Jimmy (gang member), carnival girl and, 36-37
Johnson, Sleepy, 64, 67, 73
    hiring, 81
    loyalty of, 72
    salary for, 69
Josephson, Matthew, vii

KFJZ
    fiddling contest by, 63
    playing at, 62, 65, 67
KOMA, 76

playing at, 67
KPRC, playing at, 67
KTAT
    Brown at, 68
    Gross at, 71
    playing at, 61-62, 64, 67
KVOO, v, 82
    playing at, 78, 79

Lansford, Son, 79
    hiring, 76
Light Crust Doughboys, The, vii, 65, 66
    personnel changes for, 67-68
    popularity of, 67, 69
    suit concerning, 75
Little, Bill: booking by, 73, 75

McAuliffe, Leon: hiring, 81-82
McNally, Zeb: hiring, 80-81
"Maiden's Prayer," songscript for, 94
Mayo, O. W.: booking by, 76, 77, 87
Medicine show, fiddling for, 48, 53-54, 56-64
Morrison, Samuel Eliot, ix
Music, studying, 43-44
Musicians, social standing of, 47

O'Daniel, W. Lee
    confrontation with, vii-viii, 65-66, 69-76, 78
    proposition from, 82
    support from, 70-71
    working for, 66-67, 68
Oil fields, working in, 33, 35
"Oklahoma," songscript for, 95
"On to Victory Mr. Roosevelt," 67

INDEX